The NEW Fun Encyclopedia

The NEW Fun Encyclopedia

Volume 1 Games

E. O. Harbin

revised by
Bob Sessoms

ABINGDON PRESS

Nashville

THE NEW FUN ENCYCLOPEDIA

VOLUME I. GAMES

Copyright © 1940 by Whitmore & Smith; renewed 1968 by Mary Elizabeth Harbin Standish and Thomas Harbin. Revised edition copyright © 1983 by Abingdon Press.

Second Printing 1984

Library of Congress Cataloging in Publication Data

HARBIN, E. O. (Elvin Oscar), 1885-1955
  The new fun encyclopedia.
  Rev. ed. of: The fun encyclopedia. © 1940
  Bibliography: v. 1, p.   Includes index.
  Contents: v. 1. Games— 1. Amusements—Collected works.
  2. Games—Collected works. 3. Entertaining—Collected works.
  I. Harbin, E. O. (Elvin Oscar), 1885–1955. Fun Encyclopedia.
  II. Sessoms, Bob. III. Title
GV1201.H383 1983   794   83-2818

ISBN   0-687-27754-X (v. 1)

ISBN   0-687-27755-8 (v. 2)
ISBN   0-687-27756-6 (v. 3)
ISBN   0-687-27757-4 (v. 4)
ISBN   0-687-27758-2 (v. 5)
ISBN   0-687-27759-0 (set)

MANUFACTURED BY THE PARTHENON PRESS AT
NASHVILLE, TENNESSEE, UNITED STATES OF AMERICA

CONTENTS

Part Two. The Games

INTRODUCTION

The recreational classic, *The Fun Encyclopedia* by E. O. Harbin, has assisted countless leaders of recreation in their quest for ways to help people discover and enjoy constructive and wholesome leisure activities. Volumes of writings offer the novice as well as the professional unending suggestions, but one of the leading resources has been Harbin's *Fun Encyclopedia*.

In revising this standard work, I have attempted to make this large volume more usable for everyone in the field of recreation, whether lay, professional, or academic, by dividing it into five affordable resources, each focusing on a different subject.

This is the first volume of *The New Fun Encyclopedia*. It contains many of the original games that have brought and continue to bring joy to the participants. A few older games which seemed dated by their references to bygone days have been deleted in order to present some of the newer games of today.

A section on recreation leadership is included in this first volume. It can be referred to as needed while using the other volumes. Enthusiastic leadership is essential for any successful program of recreation. It is good to review periodically the guidelines suggested by E. O. Harbin.

I have also included Harbin's "Preface" to the original one-volume edition. His suggestions and comments are as applicable today as when they were written.

The flavor which E. O. Harbin created, I have attempted to preserve; the new, I have attempted to blend into the old. May this revised edition bring as much joy to the next generation as the original brought to the past.

BOB SESSOMS

PREFACE
TO THE ORIGINAL EDITION

*T*his book is an attempt to provide in one volume a wide
variety of ideas of interesting things to do in leisure.
Suggestions are offered for home recreation, for club-
rooms, for hobbies, for banquets, for sports, for picnics, for
outings, for camps, for campfires, for hikes, for indoor and
outdoor games, for parties, for music and musical games,
for dramatics, and for puppetry. There are stories, stunts,
tricks, writing contests, quizzes, nature games, party
plans, and suggestions for almost every conceivable kind
of recreation.

No idea is of use to you until you have appropriated it,
put something of yourself into it, and put it to work. It is
the hope of the author that every reader of this book will
find some ideas that he can make his own, and that thereby
he may enrich his own life and the lives of others. Try out
some of them. Improve on them. Breathe the breath of life
into them. And see what fun it is!

It is only a partial truth that "the good things in life are
free." Most of the good things and good times of life must be
earned. This seems to be one of the laws of life. John
Ruskin said that a long time ago when he wrote: "The law
of nature is that a certain amount of work is necessary to

produce a certain quality of good. If you want knowledge you must toil for it; if food, you must toil for it; if pleasure, you must toil for it."

Capacity for the full enjoyment of life has to be developed. It involves attitudes, appreciations, interests, and skills. These do not come by happenstance or wishful thinking. They require time, patience, planning, and effort. You increase your capacity for enjoying life as you broaden and deepen your range of interests and skills. That man lives most who responds to most of the fine things about him—music, drama, art, literature, religion, creative activities, games of skill. These things need cultivation to permit proper growth. Thus one builds what L. P. Jacks refers to as "inner resources"—a sort of bank deposit of good times, a sinking fund laid up against dull moments, a reserve that is assurance that we will not be poverty stricken in ideas of what to do in free time.

Four important trends among an increasing number of leaders and institutions should be noted. We mention them briefly: (1) *The trend toward freedom of choice.* This is reflected in the increasing popularity of the open-house program where a wide variety of activities is provided. (2) *The trend toward cooperation rather than competition.* There is a feeling among a considerable number of educators and other persons interested in human welfare that the importance of competition as a factor in play has been considerably overemphasized. Some even go so far as to charge that highly organized competitive programs are deterrents to the emergence of proper social attitudes. They insist that there should be larger use made of cooperative activities and that when competitive games are used they should be promoted without the harmful stimulation that comes from tournaments, championships, and awards. "Play the game for the fun of playing" is their slogan. (3) *The trend toward creative and cultural activities.* The meaning of recreation has been broadened to include other than mere physical activities—reading, meditation, discussion, drama, music, crafts. An increasing number of clubs, schools, and churches are making use of workshop ideas, interest groups, hobby guilds. (4) *The trend toward rhythmic expression through folk games.* The growth in popularity of these games is well deserved. They are glorious fun. They are unequaled for the purpose of socializing a group. And they root back in the culture patterns of the people of many nations. This latter value is an item of no small moment in a world where there is so great a need for better understanding between peoples and races.

The writer is deeply grateful to the thousands of recreation leaders who have so profoundly influenced his own ideas of recreation and who have added to his fund of information about ways to have good times. Especially does he feel indebted to those leaders with whom he has had the privilege of sharing at the old Waldenwoods Conference, the Minnesota Recreation Leaders' Laboratory (Ihduhapi), the South-wide Leisure Time Conference, and at Lake Junaluska and Mount Sequoyah.

E. O. HARBIN
1940

The NEW Fun Encyclopedia

PART ONE

RECREATION LEADERSHIP

Before anyone can successfully lead a game, direct a drama, involve people in craft activites, or even lead a campout, there are certain basic principles that must be followed. And the leader must possess certain basic characteristics. Leadership is not necessarily a natural ability, but one that may require study and practice.

1

THE RECREATION LEADER

The following guidelines were outlined so well by E. O. Harbin that there is no need to change, adapt, or add to them. They are as vital today as when they were first published, and they should be studied, reviewed, and even become a part of the recreation leader.

SHARING VERSUS LEADERSHIP

Fun, like many of the best things in life, grows as we share it with others. This truth can be easily demonstrated: When you share a song with a comrade, or when you share a game, a book, an idea, or a skill, you both are richer for it.

It is this idea of sharing that we have in mind when we talk about the recreation leader. We are not thinking of the traffic-cop type of leader—one who *directs* leisure-time traffic into proper avenues, or frantically endeavors to do so. We need to train people, as someone has suggested, not so much for leadership as for "functioning membership."

This book, therefore, emphasizes the recreation leader *not* as a *director,* though there will be many times when directing will be necessary; *not* as a *coach,* though coaching may be necessary; *not* as a *guide,* though there may be times when the leader will point the way; but as a *sharer,* as one who has something to share with others. A sharer does not assume the teacher-pupil, or leader-follower, or counselor-counselee attitude, but the attitude of comrade and friend.

This theory of leadership will accomplish several things:

The leader

will become as inconspicuous as possible.

will not be seeking the limelight, though not afraid of it.

will become dispensable to the group and be delighted whenever it is able to proceed alone.

will not be bossy.

will not be so likely to be self-conscious.

The members of the group

will have their own ideas, skills, and talents drawn out in this sharing process.

will develop self-directive powers.

will enlarge their skill and interest range as they catch the idea of sharing.

will develop a program of wider and more varied range than would otherwise be possible.

ATTITUDES

Attitudes Toward Others

1. Cooperative—knows how to work with other people.
2. Sympathetic—is sensitive to difficulties of others.
3. Considerate—takes into account all factors involved in others' behavior; does not jump to conclusions

quickly, but is inclined to give others benefit of the doubt.

4. Unselfish—does not crave spotlight; is willing to suffer discomfort for sake of others.
5. Patient—corrects mistakes without losing temper and without embarrassing others.
6. Encouraging—offers words of commendation and helpful advice.
7. Believing—has faith in people, believes they will respond to what is good if given sufficient opportunity; believes they are cooperative; believes they have capacity and ability.

Attitudes Toward Leisure

1. Believes heartily in the necessity and benefits of play.
2. Considers the use of leisure time of prime importance in development of character and personality.
3. Sees in the wise use of leisure time a way to achieve abundant and radiant living.
4. Can properly evaluate activities in terms of their marginal and central importance, temporary and permanent value, and worth in its varying degrees.

Attitudes Toward Life

1. Is cheerful and confident, not cynical.
2. Wants to give the world a good return for its investment, does not feel the world owes one something.
3. Believes in the good life and desires that it be made available to everyone.

CHARACTERISTICS

Intellectual Character

1. Accurate, not indefinite—does not guess, digs for facts, sources.

2. Alert, not indolent—not afraid to spend mental and physical energy.
3. Retentive memory, not forgetful—develops memory by practice.
4. Keen perceptions, not unobserving.
5. Discerning, not superficial—has discriminating judgment and insight.
6. Ability to make accurate analysis, not scatter-brained.
7. Inquisitive, not lacking keen desire to know.
8. Judicious, not lacking good sense—wise and sound in decisions.
9. Thorough, not slipshod.
10. Inventive and contructive, not lacking initiative.
11. Open-minded, not dominated by prejudgment.
12. Sincere, not diverted by personal interests—when does not know, says so; makes no pretense.
13. Keen sense of values, not unresponsive to real worth.

Working Character

1. Artistic and neat, not slovenly.
2. Cooperative, not individualistic.
3. Adaptable, not slow to fit into new situations.
4. Teachable, not stubborn.
5. Efficient (definite and planned), not haphazard.
6. Attentive to details, not careless.
7. Decisive, not procrastinating.
8. Self-directive, not dependent.
9. Industrious, not lazy.
10. Prompt, not dilatory.
11. Reliable, not irresponsible or negligent.
12. Thrifty, not wasteful or extravagant.
13. Cautious, not reckless.
14. Persistent, not vacillating.
15. Cheerful, not complaining.

Personal Character

1. Conscientious, not unscrupulous.
2. Magnanimous, not small-minded and petty.
3. Self-controlled, not weak.
4. Self-respecting, not dissipated.
5. Independent, not too suggestible.
6. Thoughtful, not impulsive.
7. Prudent, not foolhardy.
8. Refined, not coarse.

Social Character

1. Faithful, not unmindful of obligations—community-minded, not narrow.
2. Helpful, not self-centered—shares, not a social sponge.
3. Loyal, not treacherous.
4. Trusting, not suspicious.
5. Just, not unfair.
6. Honest, not disposed to cheat.
7. Honorable, not sneaking.
8. Mindful of rights of others, not overbearing.
9. Sociable, not exclusive or snobbish.
10. Congenial, not unfriendly.
11. Courteous, not rude.
12. Genuine, not affected.
13. Harmonious, not antagonistic or wrangling.
14. Patient, not irritable.
15. Respectful, not impudent or flippant.
16. Tactful, not brusque or priggish.

Emotional Character

1. Courageous and self-confident, not timid—does not shirk responsibilities.
2. Ambitious, not self-satisfied.
3. Buoyant, radiant, cheerful, not morose, dull, moody.

4. Hopeful, not pessimistic.
5. Progressive, not opposed to change.
6. Earnest, not trifling.
7. Determined, not easily discouraged.
8. Idealistic, not content with low standards.
9. Responsive to beauty, not unappreciative.
10. Friendly, not lacking goodwill.
11. Grateful, not inattentive to kindness.
12. Sympathetic, not absorbed by self-interest.
13. Poised, not excitable, hysterical, or melancholy.
14. Humble, not conceited.
15. Sense of humor, not upset by trifles.
16. Forgiving, not vindictive.
17. Sportsmanlike, not envious.
18. Generous, not stingy.
19. Alive to truth, not complacent.
20. Tolerant, not angry at difference of opinion.

Physical Character

1. Developed body, not undernourished.
2. Muscular control, not clumsy.
3. Grace of figure and carriage, not slouchy.
4. Expressive face, not stolid.
5. Strong musical voice, not choked or rasping.
6. Vital, not sluggish.
7. Endurance, not easily tired.
8. Healthy, not sickly.

SKILLS

If you were to give yourself a point for each of the following skills, you could amass a total of 43 points. A score of 25 would be considered FAIR, 30—GOOD, 35—VERY GOOD, and 40 and over—EXCELLENT.

Skills in Music

1. Ability to lead a group in singing............................ 1
2. Ability to train a choir or chorus........................... 1
3. Ability to train an orchestra................................ 1
4. Ability to play a musical instrument..................... 1
5. Experience in solo, duet, quartet, or
   chorus singing... 1
6. Ability to arrange programs of music.................... 1
7. Ability to recognize at least 10 classical
   selections... 1
8. Knowledge of at least 20 folk songs.................... 1
                                             8

Skills in Dramatics

1. Ability to direct a dramatic performance............... 1
2. Ability to act a role in a performance................... 1
3. Ability to direct a group in reading and
   discussing a play.. 1
4. Knowledge of and experience with lighting,
   making sets, arranging stage settings................. 1
5. Familiarity with a wide variety of plays............... 1
6. Ability to evaluate dramatic materials................. 1
7. Knowledge of and experience with informal
   dramatics—charades, spontaneous drama,
   role-playing, etc.. 1
                                             7

Skills in Social Fellowship

1. Ability to plan and direct a party...................... 1
2. Ability to teach and lead folk games.................. 1
3. Ability to plan and direct other group games....... 1
4. Ability to help a group plan a social evening....... 1
5. Knowledge of the best source materials.............. 1
6. Knowledge of 25 social games for ready
   use in emergency.. 1
                                             6

Skills in Sports

1. Proficiency in at least one sport...............................1
2. Working knowledge of all sports...........................1
3. Ability to map out and direct a field day
   or track meet..1
4. Ability to instill in participants the idea of
   playing for the fun of playing.................................. 1
5. Accurate knowledge of field dimensions and
   rules for sports that are popular in the
   particular region.. 1

$$\overline{5}$$

Skills in Outdoor Recreation

1. Ability to plan and promote a picnic for large
   or small groups...1
2. At least elementary knowledge of nature lore—
   birds, trees, flowers, stars, etc.................................. 1
3. Ability to plan and direct interesting
   hikes and treasure hunts...1
4. Some knowledge of outdoor cookery...................... 1
5. Ability to plan and direct campfires of
   various types—council ring, campfire sing, etc..... 1
6. Knowledge of games suitable for the
   out-of-doors...1
7. Knowledge of camping...1

$$\overline{7}$$

Skills in Uses of Good Literature

1. Love for good literature and ability to
   create enthusiasm for it.. 1
2. A repertoire of good stories and ability to
   tell them...1
3. Knowledge of good poetry and ability to
   create interest in it...1

4. Ability to plan literary programs—book reviews, book discussions, poetry evenings, etc... 1
5. Ability to plan and conduct forums on interesting and timely subjects........................... 1

                                                     5

Skills in Hobbies

1. Adeptness in at least one creative hobby.............. 1
2. Wide knowledge of possible hobbies....................... 1
3. Ability to plan and conduct a hobby fair.............. 1
4. Knowledge of how to arrange for hobby classes... 1
5. A sound philosophy that discourages piddling and fadism, but encourages creativity................... 1

                                                     5

This skill rating test indicates the versatility of the recreation leader. Leadership does not necessarily require the ability to do a great variety of things well, but this test will give the leader a good idea of the points where improvement may be needed.

GENERAL REQUIREMENTS

Social Attitudes

1. Sense of the worth and dignity of every human being and desire to serve the group.
2. Understanding of people, with insight into processes of life; comprehension of hungers, needs, and aspirations of people; sense of the wholeness of life.
3. Personal realization of the joy of life, of life's rich meanings and possibilities, of the art of living.
4. Sense of humor, at least enough to prevent taking oneself too seriously.

An adequate social attitude requires familiarity with such fields as sociology, psychology, philosophy, education, history, biology, and physiology.

Creative Attitudes

1. Concern with the growth and development of each individual.
2. Concern with stimulation of creative impulses in others—initiative, freedom of expression, productive activity.

An adequate attitude requires a developed constructive faculty and creative imagination.

Scientific Attitudes

1. Understanding of the scientific method.
2. Openness to different points of view and diverse personalities.
3. Keen interest in research and experimentation.
4. Especially concerned with human engineering.

Capacity and Zest for Learning

1. An understanding mind.
2. Ability to think; skill in using the mind to analyze, to select what is significant, and to form concepts that will serve human purposes.
3. Insatiable curiosity, especially with reference to discovery and solution of social problems.

Ability to Lead Democratically

1. Belief and enthusiasm for self-government, for democracy in recreation.
2. Understanding of cooperative democratic recreation procedure, as distinguished from arbitrary control.

3. Skill in techniques of group discussion and group determination of policies.
4. Non-dominating character and personality.
5. Organizing ability.
6. Productive energy (as distinguished from mere health).

Technical Skills

1. Skill in particular field required—as executive, supervisor, specialist, or group leader, etc.
2. Skill in dealing with people according to age and group interests.

A STANDARD FOR RECREATION LEADERS

A recreation leader is very patient, maintains poise through the most trying circumstances.

A recreation leader is very kind, is particularly concerned for the slow, the careless, the indifferent.

A recreation leader knows no jealousy, is quick to pay tribute to another's skill.

A recreation leader makes no parade, never boasts of exploits and is as inconspicuous as the occasion permits.

A recreation leader assumes no airs, never pretends, never struts.

A recreation leader is never rude, respects human personality too much to treat people with anything but the greatest courtesy and considerateness.

A recreation leader is never selfish, chief concern is not "How am I doing?" but "Are all participants having a good time?"

A recreation leader is never irritated, knows that if the leader loses his or her temper and the spirit of play, how can the others be led to find it?

A recreation leader is never resentful, holds no grudge against the umpire or the other team, or the players who, by their carelessness or indifference or horseplay have made the job difficult.

A recreation leader is never glad when others go wrong, does not gloat when another recreation leader pulls a cropper, does not seize upon mistakes to hold others up to ridicule.

A recreation leader is gladdened by goodness, inspires good performance by encouraging remarks and by evident joy in the good.

A recreation leader is always slow to expose, but is alert and sees all, hears all, knows all; if someone needs discipline or help, gives it in such a way as to best benefit the individual.

A recreation leader is always eager to believe the best, looks for the best in people and always finds it.

A recreation leader is always hopeful, is not easily discouraged, embodies radiant optimism.

A recreation leader is always persevering, never gives up, endures because of firm belief.

The above is adapted and enlarged from an outline by R. C. Sidenius, Recreation and Young People's Leader of Hamilton, Ontario. It was given as a part of the worship service at a Recreation Leaders Conference held at Hamilton, Ontario, February 27, 28, 1937, sponsored by 4 F-Recreational Guild. Read I Corinthians 13:4-8.

TEN COMMANDMENTS PLUS THREE

For Those Who Toil in the Recreation Vineyard

1. Thou shalt not regard thy labors as a mere job, but as an ever-present opportunity for fine human service.
2. Thou shalt not permit thyself to get into a rut, but shalt ever be alert for new ideas the other fellow may

offer unto thee or a book may present unto thee, remembering what Mr. Matthew said of yore: "If the blind lead the blind, both shall fall in the ditch."

3. Thou shalt not forget that prompting of mere imitative motions in thy fellow humans is not, in very truth, recreation, but that evoking their inner spirit into satisfying activity is.

4. Thou shalt remember, in all thy doings, all the people within thy gates—the old as well as the young, the rich as well as the poor—for all these are in sore need of the blessings of creative expression. Deny them not, lest they shrivel and die.

5. Thou shalt open wide not merely one, or mayhap two gates of opportunity, but many—yea, all the gates through which the human mind and soul doth crave to enter in search of nourishment, understanding, and sheer delight.

6. Thou shalt never exploit innocent little children to gain vainglory for thyself nor for thy department. Neither shalt thou stir within the breasts of babes and sucklings feverish longings to gain fame and fortune in ye place called Hollywood; rather, thou shouldst provide them with nice rattles, rag dolls, and teddy bears. They are clay in thy hands, O potter!

7. Thou shalt love thy neighbor as thyself, honor the work of other well-doers in thy community, grasp their hands with cheering warmth, and join with them in mind and purpose for the greater good of all the people in thy midst—and in the doing thereof, thou shalt be mindful even of the worthy burgomaster and his trusty crew. Yea, thou shalt love, honor, and obey those whom the burgomaster hath placed over thee to guide thy footsteps and to keep thee within thy pesky budget. Yet thou shalt be

permitted to remind them gently that hope deferred maketh the heart sick!

8. Thou shalt ever keep an eagle eye on those of low repute who, for filthy lucre, would corrupt the bright imaginings and aspiring ideals of childhood and youth. With others, thou shalt up and at them, lash them hip and thigh with a whip of thorns, and put them into outer darkness now and forevermore. Thus wilt thou bring blessings unto thy people.

9. Thou who art in a high place, sometimes called boss, shalt ever lend a helping hand to the younger toilers in the vineyard, lest perchance they grow sore in spirit, tread wrong paths, step unwarily into lurking quagmires, or fall into bottomless pits; neither shalt thou smite them too rashly when they err, forgetting never that thou too wast once like unto these—just a stumbling creeper—and that in Ecclesiastes it sayeth, "Anger resteth in the bosom of fools."

10. Thou shalt not swipe the golden nuggets of thy friend's brain, over which, mayhap, that friend hath burned the midnight oil and hath sweat much gory blood. Nay, when thou wouldst use any such brain child of one who hath given it birth, thou shalt openly avow the debt and tell that friend's name unto all the people, and thou shalt set the nugget in little marks, fore and aft.

11. Thou shalt ever take heed of thine acts, especially when thou art in the marketplace where the populace may look upon thee, lest thou givest cause to thy friend to stumble and also bringest sore reproach upon thee and upon thy works. For a wise man hath said, "If you can't be glad, be careful."

12. Thou shalt ever remember the larger relationship of the work thou doest to the work like unto it, which goeth on beyond thy gates in state and nation. Yea, thou shalt cherish and strengthen such bonds, lest

thou soon findest thyself standing alone, weak and bereft, and topplest over.

13. And last, though not least, beloved of the flock, when doubts assail thee, and those of little understanding cast ridicule upon thy works, and difficulties sorely afflict thee, and thou growest weary of well-doing— oh, forget not those sources from which cometh help, refreshment, and strength of heart, for they beckon thee ever; spurn them not, but diligently use them.

—Eugene T. Lies, National Recreation Association

2

METHODS FOR THE
RECREATION LEADER

GENERAL SUGGESTIONS

Choice of Activities

1. Select activities with the following considerations in mind: age range; sex; prejudices, if any; experience, ability, and capacity of the players; size of the crowd; available play space; time allotted for play; consideration of what precedes and what follows the play period, if anything; theme, if any; possible weather conditions.
2. The leader's own knowledge and ability are determining factors, except when there are available helpers who are expert in specific activities.
3. Select games and activities with a view to giving the players a sense of successful achievement. Therefore, the activities must be within their skill range.

Arrangement of Program

1. Begin on time.
2. Start with easy activities.
3. In the early part of the program, particularly, make it easy for people to get acquainted. Break down

stiffness. Create an atmosphere of friendliness and warmth.

4. Arrange the program in logical sequence as far as possible. Each game or activity should leave players in position for the one that follows. This is not always possible, but is highly desirable.

5. Arrange for breathers. Balance the program so that the players will not be exhausted by unbroken strenuous activity.

6. Build to a fitting climax. The fun should reach its height in the closing activity.

Getting Attention

Always get everyone's attention before explaining an activity. Under no circumstances try to shout directions over the noise of an inattentive group.

1. Stand where you can easily be seen and where you can see the crowd. Do not stand in the center of the group—this is usually a poor position because part of the people will be behind you.

2. Wait for the group to become quiet before you attempt to speak. If necessary, use some signal to gain attention.

   a. Hands up! A successful method for some leaders is that of raising the right hand. As players observe this, their hands go up. It is understood that this is the signal for quiet.

   b. Shushers' Club. Some leaders say, "When my left hand goes up, every member of the Shushers' Club goes, 'Sh-sh-shush!' "

   c. Piano chord.

   d. Whistle. If you use a whistle, let it be thoroughly understood that its sound is the signal for silence, since too frequent use of a whistle is annoying. Many leaders prefer to do without it except when the game requires it. Some leaders prefer a whistle with a soft musical sound, rather than the shrill type.

e. Start a song with the aid of those closest to you. The others will join in the singing, especially if the song is familiar and tuneful. At the close of the song, or series of songs, give the group your instructions.

3. Don't dally. The moment you have the attention of the group, move with precision and snap. Delay may prove deadly.

4. Create an air of expectancy. You can do this with your manner—your enthusiasm, a merry twinkle in your eye, your evident pleasure in anticipation of the fun, the introduction of surprises, and your method of directing the activity.

Presentation of a Game and Technique During Its Progress

1. Get the group into formation before explaining the game. This makes it easier for the players to understand the directions. It also eliminates to some extent the "I-don't-want-tos" and the "I'm-not-sure-I-want-tos." They are enjoying the game before they know it. Make this procedure a part of the fun.

2. Lose as little time as possible getting into the actual playing of the game.

3. Give explanations clearly, briefly, and correctly.

4. Demonstrate. Often the very best way to explain is to take a partner or a group and demonstrate what you want done.

5. When the game is intricate or involves several movements, teach it movement by movement. Or let the players learn the game as it progresses; you can explain necessary details as you come to them.

6. Encourage the players now and then with words of commendation.
7. When mistakes are made, be patient in pointing them out; if possible, make them part of the fun. "We even enjoyed making mistakes," said one enthusiastic college student in telling about the good time he had at one party. Call attention to mistakes, but not to the persons who made them.
8. Direct attention to the game, not to yourself. A good leader merges with the group.
9. Encourage everyone to play, but do not insist that they do so. If people do not play, take it for granted that they have valid reasons.
10. When a game or activity does not catch on for some reason (the mood of the group, inability of certain players to understand, lack of time to master it) move quickly to some other game or activity. Care must be taken, however, not to destroy interest in a good activity by a poor and unsatisfactory experience with it.
11. In trying to determine the cause of the failure when a game fails to interest, first examine your own technique.
12. Stop the game while interest is at its height.
13. Be firm but kind in enforcing rules.
14. Write an outline of the things you plan to do on a small card or slip of paper. Keep this in the palm of your hand where you can refer to it if needed.
15. Have extra material ready in case of emergency. The leader may find certain games or activities impractical under the circumstances, or they may not fit the particular mood of the group. Be ready with suitable substitutes. The person who receives credit for being resourceful is very often the one who has had the foresight to prepare for emergencies.

16. Have all properties ready, but never give them out until time to use them.
17. Be thorough, but do not insist on such meticulous precision as to destroy the fun of the activity. Joy in the activity may make the participant *want* to approximate perfection.
18. Never boss, scold, or ridicule.
19. Never allow the program to drag. You must be on your toes all the time, and yet be so poised that you keep things moving with ease.
20. Enjoy the activity yourself.

PLANNING AN EVENT

Preparation

Research—Examine books, pamphlets, and magazines for ideas.

Properties—Get together all the necessary materials.

Decorations—For some events, decorations provide color, atmosphere, a festive appearance. Or exhibits may be required. Or it may be necessary to locate and prepare a suitable spot for an outdoor event. All this requires forethought and planning.

Publicity—The type of publicity will depend upon the group you want to reach. Plan interesting newspaper accounts of the coming event, letters, posters, telephone calls, announcements, and/or special invitations.

Helpers—Meet with all those who are going to help with the event and discuss jobs to be done. This is especially important when a large crowd is to be handled. Such a meeting may consist mainly of instruction.

The Crowd—Condition the people in the group for what is to come, if at all possible. Arouse interest; pique curiosity; create an atmosphere of expectancy. Then make good by fulfilling all their anticipations, and more.

Know their likes and dislikes, and the reasons for them. Know their needs, felt and unfelt. Know their background. Keep all these things in mind while planning the event.

Guiding Principles

Unity—Unity will be easier to achieve if the aim of the particular program is clear. For instance, one college wanted to interest its students in a varied campus social program. One of their events was A World Play Day held in connection with a homecoming celebration. A variety of activities took place—speeches, folk games on the athletic field, a football game, etc. But through it all, they kept the main purpose in view, and thus the day's program was a unit. Sometimes unity is achieved by using a theme for the whole program: Hobby Fair, Circus Party, Nature Hike, Council Campfire, Evening of Indian Music, or Drama Festival.

Variety—Not only should there be variety in particular events, but each group should be given a variety of experiences over a period of time. A chance to enjoy experiences with drama, music, parties, forums, sports, hobbies, and all the other interests that make up a well-rounded life should get into the picture at one time or another.

Someone has suggested facetiously that a lullaby puts a baby to sleep because of the dreadful monotony of the thing. Certainly no group can afford to lull its crowd to sleep with a monotonous sameness in the events it promotes. There must be an element of surprise, the lure of new ventures, the tang of an occasional new idea, the pull of opening horizons.

Climax—The event, whether it be a banquet, a musicale, or a party, should reach a fitting climax. Save the best for last: a banquet feature that caps the program for the evening, a musical number that marks the interest peak for the night, a game or stunt that finds the fun at its highest level. Sometimes a surprise can serve as this climax. Sometimes a sing can do it by drawing the threads of fellowship together in a closing moment of harmony. Sometimes a lovely experience, such as a beautiful story that fits the theme, or a brief worship experience, can mark the climax. Whatever it is, build to a climax—and stop!

WORKING WITH A COMMITTEE

Usually recreation plans are most successful when they represent the pooled thoughts of a committee. "Everybody knows more than anybody does." Combined thinking is likely to result in bigger and better plans than one person alone could devise.

Important Rules for Successful Committee Meetings

1. Be prompt in beginning and closing the sessions.
2. Stick to the business to be done. Don't wander off into more or less interesting bypaths unrelated to the job.
3. Move with precision. When a point of progress has been made, clinch it and move on to the next item.
4. When ideas of different members are at variance, try to find some points of agreement and work from those.
5. Encourage every member to participate in the discussions. Give respectful consideration to each suggestion. Even weak suggestions can often be used. Point out whatever good is in them and build on that. Never ridicule any suggestion given in good faith.
6. Discourage any attempt on the part of one person to dominate the decisions of the group. The chair must be particularly careful not to abuse the authority of that position in committee deliberations.
7. Often the committee meetings can be occasions for good fellowship. Some light refreshments, a trying-

out of materials to be used later in programs, or a meeting in connection with an attractive meal can put the members in the mood to do some good work. Care needs to be taken, however, that the social aspects of the meeting do not interfere with the business at hand.

8. The chairperson has much to do with the successful functioning of a committee. He or she must be fair, alert, thorough, systematic, humble, open-minded, and tactful. There are three types of committee chairpersons. For two of these, success is impossible unless the other members take things into their own hands.

   a. The empty-headed chairperson has given the meeting no previous thought and has no ideas. If the other members of the committee are like this one, the session reaches a stalemate. "Well, we've got to do *something!*" And the result is a flat, stereotyped plan.

   b. The rubber-stamp chairperson has everything all planned. He or she *tells* the committee and does not receive suggestions cordially unless they coincide with those prepared plans. The committee is used merely as a rubber stamp. Its members feel their time has been wasted. The chair could have done without them.

   c. The good chairperson has given serious thought to the committee meeting: has jotted down an agenda of things that need to be done, has encouraged the members to bring ideas to throw into the hopper, and may even have given them some material so that they may examine it for suggestions. He or she has some ideas, but does not insist on them. This chairperson thinks *with* the committee, not *for* it. The plans that are worked up are the *committee's* plans.

CRITERIA FOR EVALUATING THE PROGRAM

1. Is the program a result of democratic participation by those involved in determining its content?
2. Does it take into account the potential, as well as the present interests of the group?
3. Does it overemphasize the value of temporary interests, as compared to permanent interest?
4. Does it set in motion any new and growing interests?
5. Does it provide any means for following up such interests?
6. Is there definite advancement in skills and appreciation as a result of the activities?
7. Is the group becoming more skillful and versatile in the art of leisure, so that the members are no longer easy victims of fruitless patterns of play?
8. Are the creative abilities of the participants challenged and given opportunity to develop?
9. Does the program develop a spirit of friendliness? Is anyone left out of the circle of friendship?
10. What contribution, if any, has the program made toward participants' development of well-rounded personalities?
11. What disintegrating personality factors, if any, has it set in motion? Has any bad feeling been aroused? Jealousy? Bitterness? Division? Desire for self-display? Inflated ideas of importance?
12. Does the program make the best use of the equipment, leadership, and time available? And does it challenge the talents and capacities of the participants?

ENCOURAGING PARTICIPATION

Fingerprint experts testify that no two people have identical fingerprints. It is doubtful whether any two people are exactly alike in their attitudes and responses. To a certain extent, people can be classified in groups, but within each type of group, there are individuals. It is important that this be kept in mind in trying to solve the problems related to obtaining participation. The recreation leader must study the individuals.

Often there is also a difference in communities and neighborhoods. Recreation plans that "strike fire" in one community often "backfire" in another. Mental, physical, and moral background, traditional attitudes, and past experiences are factors in these differences. The recreation leader must take these into account, studying each individual's environment.

The leader is concerned with more than whether people engage in the activities. He or she wants them to find their own best selves through the release and enrichment that comes from those activities.

Certain types of individuals are fairly common in the experience of the recreation leader. A few are noted here, with some suggestions that may help them.

The Timid, Backward, Bashful

The Problem—Restrained participation prevents spontaneous play. They appear to be antisocial when they really would rather be friendly.

Possible Causes—Lack of experience in the activity makes them fear embarrassment. Self-consciousness makes it difficult to mingle. Unsympathetic people in the group make "smart" remarks about participants, or make the timid the butt of their alleged jokes. The leader continually plays "tricks" on participants.

Ways to Help—Find something the timid can do well and assign it to them. Seek tasks for them where they will not be conspicuous. Offer an encouraging word occasionally. Always be sympathetic. Never make them the victim of "goat stunts." Develop a friendly spirit in the group, making it easier for the timid and inexperienced to participate without embarrassment. Encourage small-group socials to help break the ice.

The Lovelorn

The Problem—Couples prefer to "sit out." They resent being separated in games. They are extremely unsocial.

Possible Causes—Cozy corners in the social room invite "sitting out." They fear not doing well in the eyes of the beloved. A sort of "superiority complex" sometimes characterizes lovesick couples. They desire to impress each other with the idea that the other's company is all in the world that is necessary for complete happiness. Lack of program continuity makes it necessary for people to entertain themselves. Automobiles make it easy to "sit out" or leave for a ride.

Ways to Help—Eliminate all cozy corners as far as possible. Keep the program moving. Use games that mix the group. Use clever devices for choosing partners, but allow no partner arrangement to last longer than one or two games. Create sentiment against the use of automobiles during the activities. Plan such an interesting party that everyone will want to participate.

The Dignified

The Problem—They participate only reluctantly and with an "I'm doing you a big favor" air. They have a depressing effect on the rest of the group.

Possible Causes—They feel that play is silly and intended only for children. They fear that the group's estimate of them would be lowered if they "let loose." They feel that play is unbecoming in those with serious purposes in life. They have an exaggerated personal pride that objects to engaging in anything in which they do not excel.

Ways to Help—Educate them in the importance of play. Seek to arouse their play spirit by discovering something they like to do—perhaps sing, debate, or act. Develop programs of such high quality that they are forced to see the value in them.

The Religious Dyspeptic

The Problem—They disapprove of harmless fun and sometimes are very critical. They have a depressing effect on the rest of the group.

Possible Causes—Actions of some people in the group are subject to criticism. The committee has allowed objectionable features to creep into the programs. They feel that play is evil, a sinful waste of time, and dangerous to the spiritual life. Commercialized amusements and other agencies in the community offer harmful types of recreation and thus arouse antagonism toward all forms of leisure time activity.

Ways to Help—Educate them in the values of wholesome play. Demonstrate those values by actual promotion of such recreation. Have respect for their sincere convictions.

The Know-It-All

The Problem—They lessen interest of players by disparaging remarks: "Oh, I know that." "That's an old one." "Why don't we try something new?" They take edge off a game when they explain it to players around them while leader is trying to give directions to group.

Possible Causes—The committee or leader uses too much "old stuff." Their exaggerated case of egos resent having it appear that anyone knows more than they do. There is a clique with which the "know-it-alls" have influence.

Ways to Help—Use them in places of leadership, if possible. Use new material in your programs. Don't assume a know-it-all attitude yourself. The more one knows, the more conscious one is that there is much to be learned. Make them victims of "goat" stunts occasionally. Never do this with malice, however.

The Blasé

The Problem—They participate only reluctantly and with a bored air. Their attitude proves a deterring factor in games or other activities.

Possible Causes—They have an excessive enthusiasm for social dancing, so that nothing else appears worth doing. They desire to appear sophisticated. There is a lack of variety in the programs. There is too much "kid stuff" in programs.

Ways to Help—Use new material in programs. Make the party programs lively and interesting. Don't coddle. Introduce surprises in programs. Occasionally use them as victims for "goat" stunts.

The Grandstand Type

The Problem—Desire to be prominent in all activities. Sometimes seek to start something else while leader is directing an activity. "Smart" remarks are a disturbing factor.

Possible Causes—A lack of continuity in the program gives the grandstand players opportunity to take the reins. The leadership allows the more aggressive to "hog" the program. There is a group feeling of dissatisfaction with the leadership and the program.

Ways to Help—Have a well-planned program with no awkward pauses. Strive to give everyone a chance in games. Occasionally give the grandstander some responsibility in the program. Use them as victims in "goat" stunts.

Objectors

The Problem—They oppose the plans of committee or suggestions of leader. Some people seem to have been born in the "objective case." The play spirit of the group is dissipated by disparaging remarks: "Oh, let's not do that. Let's do so-and-so."

Possible Causes—There is lack of confidence on the part of the leader. There is lack of enthusiasm on the part of the leader. There is lack of friendliness in the group. Ill feeling or envy always gives rise to a flock of problems. There is a desire on the part of the objector to dominate the group.

Ways to Help—Consult with the committee in planning, so that the program does not represent only the leader's ideas. Maybe the objectors have much to be said in their favor. If the objectors' suggestions seem good, it may be possible to use them. The leader ought never to wear that "I'm infallible" air. Sometimes the leader should say, "All right. Let's play this one now, and then we'll play the one you suggested." Always be courteous, but don't spoil the plans arranged by the committee by acquiescing to every suggestion after the games are started. Sometimes it is advisable to ignore a chronic objector.

The Lazy

The Problem—They participate only reluctantly and so listlessly as to prove a hindrance to the game.

Possible Causes—Programs are too strenuous. They feel that recreation is simply resting. Hard work has left their energies too depleted for much physical activity in play. They may have poor health.

Ways to Help—Adapt the program to the physical needs of the group. Encourage the lazy to play, but don't nag.

The Mentally Handicapped

The Problem—They don't know how to play. A weakened mental state is often accompanied by physical weakness, depleted energies, and lack of interest, so that it is difficult to arouse a spontaneous play spirit.

Possible Causes—Those in charge may not know the value of play as a mental and physical stimulant. Leadership may be unsympathetic.

Ways to Help—Plan simple games. Have infinite patience. Find something the persons with retardation can do well and build on that. Experiment with music in participating and nonparticipating programs. Songs and other musical activities provide relaxing, entertaining, and enjoyable experiences.

Other Ways to Gain Participation

1. Never be overly insistent that any person participate.
2. Have confidence in the power of suggestion. The play spirit is contagious. Often it is best to go ahead and play, ignoring any special problems.
3. Always remember that you may be mistaken in your analysis of the situation. The player you classify as lazy may be in poor health. The person you tag grandstand player may simply be interested in making the program go.
4. Don't offer public criticism of any player.
5. Maintain your poise under all conditions. The slogan for a successful recreation leader—Say It with a Smile.
6. Be sympathetic with any difficulties the players may have.

SOME QUESTIONS FOR THE LEADER

1. Am I friendly and congenial?
2. Have I tried to discover my own interests and abilities, and do I try to develop those interests and abilities?

3. Do I refrain from unnecessarily hurting the feelings of others?
4. Am I familiar with the rules of common courtesy and good manners?
5. Do I watch for every opportunity to do a kindness?
6. Do I recognize my obligations to my organization?
7. Do I put cooperation before competition?
8. Do I respect another's viewpoint?
9. Do I suggest, rather than command or demand?
10. Do I try to remedy a bad situation rather than just complaining?
11. Do I conceal unpleasant feelings?
12. Do I give credit where and when credit is due?
13. Do I take advantage of opportunities to develop my self-confidence?
14. Do I read widely?
15. Do I endeavor to overcome objectionable mannerisms?
16. Do I make an effort to understand the situation or problem with which I am confronted?
17. Do I try to foresee possible results?
18. Do I try to avoid prejudice or bias in my thinking?
19. Do I recognize the value of facts?
20. Am I always on the alert to improve my plans?
21. Do I take advantage of opportunities to learn more about my field?
22. Do I remain poised under criticism? Do I profit by criticism?
23. Do I check on myself when a project has not been a success, to discover whether I was at fault?
24. Do I look at myself objectively to find my strong points and weak points? Do I do anything about what I find?
25. Do I plan my work carefully, or do I simply trust to the inspiration of the moment?

—Adapted from BRUCE TOM

GUIDELINES

In planning games, the recreation leader should be aware of certain guidelines. I will repeat here many of the suggestions already given, since they cannot be emphasized too strongly.

1. Research to find games that are best suited for the occasion, the general age of the group, the sex of the group (all female, all male, or mixed), and to be certain the games are not too difficult for that particular group.
2. Always plan more games than you will need.
3. Set up the game area (court, room, field) before the event is to take place.
4. Have at hand all the materials you will need.
5. Plan something for the early arriver.
6. Begin on time.
7. Mix active and inactive games. Don't tire out your guests too soon.
8. Know the rules of the games by heart. But keep your resource cards handy.
9. Stand where you can be seen and heard. It is best not to stand in the center of a circle, but as part of the circle itself. Do not shout. Talk in a normal tone after you have everyone's attention.
10. Describe the rules of the game thoroughly.
11. DEMONSTRATE! After the rules have been explained, have a trial run to demonstrate the game.
12. End a game at the peak of fun. Don't drag it on and on. People will want to play that game again if they enjoy it. If it becomes boring, they will not want to play it the next time you plan to use it.
13. End on time! Don't keep people longer than they expect to be there. It is not necessary to use all the activities you have planned. Let them leave wanting more. They will want to come back!

The following games will provide a mixture of ideas and fun. It is up to you, the leader, to plan and provide the very best in wholesome entertainment for your guests. Enjoy their enjoyment; laugh with their laughter; explode with their explosions of release. You are a vital part of their fun, but *they* are the ones who are important—not you. Without them, you could not have a game; they are the reason for playing. But you make or break a game by your attitude and your enthusiasm. Capture the moment and create life!

PART TWO

THE GAMES

Games—those fun activities that help us escape into a world of frolic, laughter, renewal, refreshment, and relaxation. Games—those sometime crazy activities that help us to just have fun, to just have joy, to just have a moment of pleasure. For some, games can teach; for others, games are therapy. For whatever use, games do have a purpose.

3

FUN WITH ICEBREAKERS

Icebreakers are those introductory games that help mix the crowd, set the mood, create the atmosphere, establish the attitude of play, and just about make or break the entire occasion. Plan with finesse and purpose! Lead with grace and authority!

MIXERS

May We Introduce—At a party for married couples, hand out mimeographed sheets and ask each couple to complete the following information.

1. This is Mr. & Mrs. _____
2. They met at _____
3. They were married on (date) _____
4. They honeymooned in _____
5. They have _____ children.
6. Their hobbies are _____
7. They enjoy _____

After all the sheets have been turned in, ask each couple to stand as their information is read to the group.

Choo-choo—Players form a circle. One player stands inside the circle in front of one of the other players, introduces him or herself to that player, and then asks, "What is your name?" That player may say, "Stella Smith." The center player then jumps in place in front of "Stella." This is done in rhythm five times, first right foot and right hand extended toward the player, then left foot and left hand, then right, left, right. On each jump the name is repeated: "Stella! Stella! Stella, Stella, Stella!" The player then turns away, Stella puts her hands on his or her shoulders, and they begin "choo-chooing" inside the circle until they stop in front of another player. Again there is the introduction, the jumping and the repeating of the name, this time by two people. Now player Number One and Stella turn, Number One holds Stella's shoulders, Number Three puts his or her hands on Number One's shoulders, and the three of them Choo-Choo to a fourth player. Each time the group reverses after the jumping, so that a new player becomes leader.

In a large crowd, the number of starters can be increased, so that there may be from three to ten "trains" operating at one time. This is a good way to divide the crowd into teams for games or stunts that are to follow.

Introductions—Each person is given a card, with the name of another guest. The person must find that guest, introduce him or herself, and fill in the blanks on the cards.

Name _____*John Jones*_____

Hobby _____

Disposition _____

Color of eyes _____

After the cards are turned in, they may be redistributed and read aloud.

Bumpety-bump-bump—This is a good get-acquainted game. It also serves to keep the players alert. One player in the center points to someone in the circle and says, "Right! Bumpety-bump-bump!" The person to whom the center player points must shout the name of the person on his or her right before the player finishes speaking, or take the center player's place. In a large group, there may be several center players.

Howdy—This is an old favorite, played like Bingo. Before the event, prepare cards like this example:

H	O	W	D	Y

Upon arrival, each guest signs a piece of paper, places it in a container, and is given a HOWDY card and a pencil. The guests are to sign their names in the spaces of one another's cards until all the cards are filled. No one can sign the same card twice. Upon completing their cards, the guests sit down. When all are seated, pull the names from the container one at a time and call them out. The guests are to cross the names off their HOWDY cards. The first person to cross off five names in a vertical, horizontal, or diagonal row shouts HOWDY!

Variation: When a name is called, that person must stand and tell something about him or herself.

Famous People—As guests arrive, tag them with the names of famous people—Bible characters, historic personages, characters in fiction or literature, movie stars, athletes, political figures. March in concentric circles, one circle marching counterclockwise and the other clockwise. When the music stops, each person faces someone in the other circle, notes the name, and makes appropriate greeting. They may indulge in a moment of conversation, asking questions or engaging in banter. For instance, Jezebel meets David and the following conversation ensues: "How do you do, David? Where is your harp? Did you bring your sling?" "And how are you, Jezebel? How does it feel to be pitched out a window?"

When the music starts again they yell, "Goodbye!" and move on to meet some other famous person.

The names can be used all evening, no matter what games are played.

Right Face, Left Face—Everyone sits in a circle. A person chosen to be It walks around the circle, points to a player, and says either, "Right Face!" or "Left Face!" Before It counts to ten, the player is to say the name of either the person on the right or the one on the left. On failing, the player becomes It. If It says "Attention!" the player is to give his or her own name.

Memory—All guests receive name tags as they arrive. Within a certain time limit, they are to memorize as many names of other guests as possible. Then they all sit down and remove their name tags. They are given pencils and paper and are to write down as many names as they can remember. After five minutes, the one with the most names wins.

Conversation Circle—Players march in concentric circles in opposite directions, boys on the inside and girls on the outside. When the leader blows a whistle or horn, they stop and face each other. Players directly opposite each other discuss whatever topic the leader calls. Some suggested topics:

What is your favorite TV program?
What do you think of the present-day space attempts?
What do you think of the present-day fashions?
What do you think of the world situation?
What is the best book you've ever read?
What is the best magazine article you have read recently?
What good movie have you seen recently?
What is your favorite group?
What is your favorite football team, basketball team?
What is your favorite flower?

Paper Bag Introduction—Guests are provided with crayons and paper bags. Each must draw a face on the bag. Noses and ears may be added by the use of some extra paper and paste. Curls may be added in the same manner. These paper bag puppets are now tied on the right hand and guests and puppets greet one another. Impromptu puppet shows may result. For this game, provide a work table with all the necessary supplies available.

A Name Plus—Everyone sits in a circle. The leader says his or her name aloud. The player next to the leader must repeat the leader's name, and then say his or her own name. The third player repeats the names of the leader and the first player, then adds his or her own name. This goes around the entire circle until the last player has called out everyone's name, including his or her own.

Advertisement—Cut trade names out of newspapers and magazines—Puppy Chow, Chevrolet, etc. Then cut the letters apart and place each name in an envelope. Give an envelope to each guest. The guests are to unscramble the letters to discover their trade names. They then write the names on name tags and wear them during the evening.

Baby Who?—Ask all guests to bring baby pictures of themselves. Identify each picture with a number. Place all photographs on a bulletin board, with the number under each. Give the guests pencil and paper and have them try to match as many pictures as possible with their owners.

An Acrostic—Hand each guest a pencil and a sheet of paper with these written instructions: Print your first name vertically in capital letters on the left side of the paper. Then circulate among the guests and find people whose first names begin with the letters in your first name. Write their names beside the letters in your name. No name may be used twice. Sit down when you have completed the list. Example: Ricky
Opal
Beth
Betty
Ivan
Edith

Autograph Hunt—Mimeograph this questionnaire and hand one copy and a pencil to each guest. Ask them to find people who fit the descriptions. Guests sit down when all the spaces are filled.

1. Someone born in another state _____
2. Someone wearing contact lenses _____
3. Someone wearing blue jeans _____
4. Someone who has traveled outside the USA __
5. Someone with pierced ears _____
6. Someone born in the same month as you ____
7. Someone with a credit card _____
8. Someone with a calendar watch _____
9. Someone with light-colored socks _____
10. Someone who doesn't like to fly _____
11. Someone who plays a musical instrument ___
12. Someone who likes grits _____
13. Someone who is over 30 _____
14. Someone who has a mustache _____
15. Someone who doesn't watch TV _____
16. Someone who doesn't eat breakfast _____
17. Someone who plays tennis _____
18. Someone who is wearing a diamond ring ___
19. Someone who snores _____
20. Someone who is wearing shoes that tie _____

I've Got Your Number—Give each guest a large paper number to be worn throughout the game. Now give each person a slip with different instructions. Example:

Introduce 4 to 3; shake hands with 6 and 7; go to 10 and shake hands 3 ways—Chinese fashion (each shakes own hand), society grip (hands held high), and good old pump-handle shake; kneel before 12 and meow 3 times; find out the color of 11's eyes; ask 7 what is best for breakfast; ask 2 why good men are hard to find.

Zip—Players sit in chairs in a circle. Each person must learn the name of the person on his or her left. It, in the center, points to anyone in the circle and says, "One, two, three, four, five, Zip!" The player to whom It is pointing must shout the name of the person on his or her left before Zip! is called. Failing to do this, the player must exchange places with It. The game must move rapidly. There may be several "zippers" in the center of the circle.

When a center player shouts, "Boom-Zip! *all* players must change seats. In the ensuing scramble the zippers may get seats. Players must become acquainted rapidly with their new left-hand neighbors, for a zipper may be along at any moment.

Variation: The word Zap! can be used to identify the person on the *right*. "It" calls either Zip! or Zap! and the player pointed to must identify either the person on the left or the one on the right before It counts 10. Failing to do this, the player becomes It.

Spiral Handshake—The guests "grand march" into a spiral. Then the center player starts handshaking his or her way out of the spiral. This player, Number One, must shake hands with each player in turn, then stand in line and wait for the rest of the crowd to come by. As number one passes the player next to him or her, that player follows number one around the spiral. So each player shakes hands with all the other players twice—once when he or she passes them, and again when they pass.

Sack Shake—Tie a paper bag on the right hand of each guest. Request that they move about shaking hands, while trying to keep the paper bag in good condition. Each person must keep a count of the number of hands shaken. At the end, simple prizes are given to the person who has shaken the most hands, and to the one who has least battered paper bag.

Complete My Name—Ask the guests to print their name tags, leaving out the vowels. Give pencils and paper. The guests are to try to complete the names by filling in the vowels. Example: Robert Beasley would look like R__B__RT B__ __SL__ __. If members of the group know one another well, substitute names of famous people.

FINDING PARTNERS AND FORMING GROUPS

Hand Out—Girls stand behind a screen. One at a time, they put out a hand. As a hand appears, a boy steps up and leads the owner of the hand away as his partner.

Athlete's Foot—Boys stand behind a sheet with only their feet showing. Girls select their partners by pointing out the pair of feet wanted.

Pulling Strings—Long strings pass through a large heart (hoop, target, paper turkey, paper football) and hang down on either side. Girls take hold of the ends on one side and boys on the other. At a signal, they pull and locate their partners. Care must be taken that the number of strings corresponds with the number of people present.

Shadow Auction—Either the boys or the girls stand behind a shadow screen and are sold at auction—beans, counters, or pins may be used. Subjects may disguise their appearance with false noses, ears, or hair.

Missing Pieces—Use this mixer at seasonal times of the year to divide a large group into smaller groups of 4 to 6 people. Cut valentines, Christmas cards, or birthday cards into 4 or 6 pieces, depending on the number of people desired in each group. Mix all the pieces together and place in a box. Have each guest take one piece of a card. The small groups will be formed as the guests locate the missing pieces and put their card back together.

Secret Couples—Guests' names are put into two boxes— one for girls and one for boys. The King and Queen of Hearts (or King and Queen of Hunky Bunky or George and Martha Washington) preside over this affair. They draw 5 or 6 names from each box—the King draws girls' names and the Queen draws boys' names. The King and Queen secretly pair these names and label the couples:

(1) The most sensible couple.
(2) The most handsome couple.
(3) The most brilliant couple.
(4) The most thrifty couple.
(5) The most lovable couple.
(6) The most popular couple.

Guests pair off and appear before the throne to find out if they are "the most of this or that" couple. If properly paired, they stay partners and due announcement is made. If not, they immediately leave the throne and each brings up another partner.

Riddle Partners—Each boy is provided with a riddle. Each girl draws an answer from a container. Each boy tries to find the answer to his riddle. The girl who has the answer becomes his partner for the next event.

Variations: (a) **Famous People Reminders**—The boys are given slips with the names of famous people. The girls draw slips telling something that will remind them of a particular character. Examples:

Moses . . . the burning bush
George Washington . . . hatchet
Lincoln . . . rail splitter
Betsy Ross . . . flag

(b) **Affinities**—Give each boy one word of an affinity and each girl another. Examples:

Jack and *Jill*	Anthony and *Cleopatra*
Salt and *Pepper*	Ham and *Eggs*
Ice Cream and *Cake*	Lock and *Key*
Thunder and *Lightning*	Soap and *Water*
Bread and *Butter*	Knife and *Fork*
Pen and *Ink*	Brush and *Comb*
Light and *Dark*	Good and *Evil*
Cup and *Saucer*	Bow and *Arrow*
Hit and *Run*	Army and *Navy*
Cream and *Sugar*	Day and *Night*

(c) **Completing Quotations**—Give the girls the first part of the quotation and the boys the last. The girl who has "Strong as an" looks for the boy who has "Ox." Other suggestions:

Sweet as *Sugar*	Sour as *Vinegar*
Hot as *Blazes*	Tough as *Shoe Leather*
Hard as *Rock*	Thin as a *Rail*
Light as a *Feather*	Fast as *Lightning*
Cold as *Ice*	Quiet as a *Mouse*
Green as *Grass*	Sly as a *Fox*
Slow as *Molasses*	Neat as a *Pin*
Heavy as *Lead*	Slippery as an *Eel*
Proud as a *Peacock*	Fit as a *Fiddle*
Stiff as a *Board*	Busy as a *Bee*
Flat as a *Pancake*	Dead as a *Doornail*

(d) **Definitions**—Write words on one set of slips and their definitions on another set. Let the women draw the definitions and the men the words. Each definition looks for its word. Thus the woman with "The last letter in the Greek alphabet" would look for the man with "Omega." "A drama wholly or mostly sung, with orchestral accompaniment and appropriate costumes, scenery, and action" would pair off with "Opera." The dictionary will furnish a sufficient number of words to answer your purpose.

Clap In, Clap Out—The boys are taken out of the room and numbered. The girls form a circle standing behind chairs. Now one of the girls calls a number. The boy with that number enters the room. He tries to guess who called his number and sits in that girl's chair. If he is wrong the girls applaud. He keeps on trying until he finally gets the right chair. The silence indicates to him that he is correct. He remains seated. Another boy is called in. And so it goes until all boys have been called and have found the girls who called their numbers. This would make a good game to pair off couples for some game that is to follow.

Variation: Instead of numbering the boys, have the girls call them by name.

Where Are You?—As guests arrive, have each write his or her name on a name tag. Arrange chairs in a circle, one chair for each guest. As music plays, the guests walk around the chairs. When the music stops, they drop their name tags on the nearest chair. The music begins and the guests again walk around the chairs. When the music stops, each guest picks up the name tag on the nearest chair and begins to look for that person.

Animal Sounds—To form groups, hand each guest a piece of paper with the name of an animal on it. The number of animals will depend on the number of groups needed for the evening of games. At the beginning of a game, guests are to imitate the sound of the animal listed on their papers. They are to find others who are making similar sounds.

Gathering Nuts—To form groups, give the guests name tags in the shape of different nuts—walnut, peanut, pecan, etc. At a signal, they are to find other guests who have the same nut name tag.

Fish Pond—Girls hide behind a screen. Boys drop a fishing line over the screen. Some girl takes hold and walks out to be the boy's partner.

Chairless Couples—Two sets of chairs are arranged as for Going to Jerusalem. Boys form a circle around one set and girls around the other. In each set there is one less chair than there are persons. As the music starts the players march around the chairs. When it stops each person tries to get a chair. The boy and girl left out become partners for the next event. Each time players drop out chairs are removed. This continues until all the players have partners.

Song Scramble—Give each guest a slip of paper containing one line of a song. The players then scramble around trying to find the other lines of their song. When all the song groups are complete, they must render their songs. Perhaps each member of the group could sing his or her own line.

OTHER GOOD INTRODUCTORY GAMES

Bean Quiz—When the guests arrive, give each person 10 beans, with instructions as to how to proceed. Whenever a person is tricked into answering Yes or No to a question, that person surrenders one bean to the questioner. At the end, the winner is the person holding the largest number of beans. The game may continue throughout a whole evening.

Variation: Bells, candles, and the like may be used instead of beans.

You Have a Face—Players are seated in a circle. The leader announces that all answers must be made with words beginning with the letter *C,* and that no word can be used twice. One player turns to the neighbor on the right and says, "You have a face." The neighbor responds, "What kind of face?" "Cheerful face," says the first player. This player turns to the player on the right and the game proceeds: "Cherub face," "calm face," "comical face," "cosmetic face," etc. It's fun to see just how long one letter can be used. The leader may designate any letter.

Variation: Using the same procedure, pass a compliment to the neighbor.

Laugh—Players are seated in a circle. The first player starts by saying, "Ha." The second player says, "Ha, Ha." The third says, "Ha, Ha, Ha." And so it goes around the circle, each player adding another Ha. In each case the Has must be pronounced solemnly, on pain of dismissal from the circle. The chances are, however, that it will not get around the circle before the entire group is responding with gales of laughter.

Laughing Hat—Divide into two teams. Toss a hat into the air. If it lands top side up, one team laughs immediately. If it lands bottom side up, the other team laughs. Any player failing to laugh must drop out.

Rummage—Guests are asked to bring along some old clothing—hats, shoes, dresses, coats, etc.—which later will be given to the needy. They all stand in a circle with their bundles. The music starts, and the bundles are passed to the right. When the music stops or the whistle blows, the guests open the bundles they have at the time. They then don the garments and wear them for the rest of the evening.

White Elephants—Guests are asked to bring something for which they no longer have any use. They may wrap these white elephants in any manner they choose. Guests draw numbers to determine in what order they are to choose a white elephant. The last person takes whatever is left. After all the guests have their packages they may open them. If not satisfied, they may wrap them up again and try to trade with someone.

Variations: (a) Guests number off consecutively—1, 2, 3, etc. Number One gets up, chooses a package, opens it, sits down. Number Two can do the same, *or* Number Two can choose Number One's package instead. If so, Number One goes back to choose another gift. The game continues as each person chooses a gift, opens it, and so on. A gift may be exchanged only three times, at which time it is "frozen." Sometimes called **Chinese Auction**.

(b) Guests are given numbers and a different number is placed on the packages they have brought. As the leader calls out the numbers, each player must find the package with his or her number on it.

(c) Place all the parcels on a table and tie a long string around each one. A covering is placed over the packages, with the strings hanging down in view. In turn, each guest goes to the table and pulls a string to find a package.

Pocketbook Scavenger Hunt—The men will have to get out their wallets and the women their purses for this game. Divide into groups. As the leader calls out each item, the first one to visibly show the item receives a point for that group. Some suggested items: car keys, chewing gum, emory board, lipstick, safety pin, pocket knife, credit card, etc. The winning team is the one with the most points.

Jumbled Words Charades—Write out words and cut them into single letters, giving the same number to each letter of a given word. Pass these letters out and have the players get together with the others who have the same number on their letters. The players in each group try to discover what their word is, and then they act it out for the other groups to guess. For example, all the number 1s get together and find that they have 8 letters: L, L, B, S, E, A, A, B. They put their letters down and take a look at them. Finally, someone suggests that their word is Baseball. Then they act it out.

Cobweb Mixer—After all the guests have arrived, they are led to a corner of the room where there is a giant cobweb made of strings. Within easy reach, near the center of the web, are loose strings. Each person is to take a string and follow it to the end. It will go down to the bottom of the web, then along the floor, over chairs, upstairs, downstairs, through hallways, perhaps crossing, looping, and tangling with other strings. The players will stop to untangle their strings, and often several players will work together at the same point. When they come to the end, there should be some prize—a trinket of some sort, a fortune written on a slip of paper, or directions for the next event (instructions to get together with certain others to prepare a stunt, explanation of a game to be played, or the title of a song to be sung).

Professions—Choose partners by drawing numbers or in some other way. Partners draw from a container a slip of paper on which is written some profession or occupation—lawyer, teacher, doctor, actor, announcer, politician, chemist, concert artist, opera star, etc. Partners must then act out the profession while the rest try to guess what it is. For instance, the "dentist" pulls a tooth for the patient, or fills one.

Shoe Scramble—All players take off their shoes. They are stacked in a pile at center, being mixed around in the

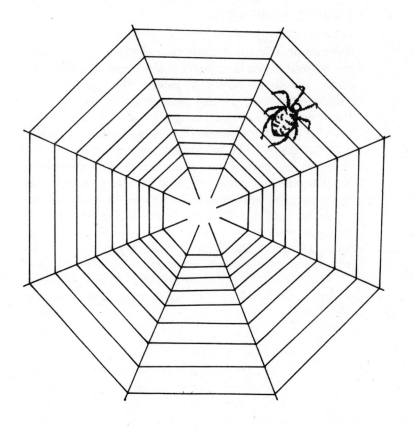

Cobweb Mixer

process. At a signal, all players rush to put on their shoes. The last 3 or 4 players to finish may be required to perform some stunt for the group.

Impromptu Circus—Guests draw slips from a container. These slips indicate their parts in the circus. There will be clowns, acrobats, bareback riders, the circus band, animals (elephants, giraffes, monkeys, lions, dogs). After all the guests have joined their groups, each group is given 10 or 15 minutes to organize its part in the show, and then the circus begins. The leader acts as ringmaster.

A bit of previous planning can add to the effectiveness of the performance. It would be good to have on hand some properties to be used by the performers—clown suits and false faces, makeup, hobbyhorses or sticks, kazoos and other instruments, blankets, stuffed stockings for elephant trunks, brooms for giraffe necks, paper and cardboard to make animal heads, and other material of this sort. These could be hidden about the room, and part of the fun could be that each group must find its own equipment.

A Masque of Months—Organize the group by birthday months: All the January people get together, all the February, and so on. After a few moments for consultation and planning, the show is on. January could stage a snowball fight with handkerchiefs. February could celebrate any one of a few birthdays—Washington, Lincoln, Longfellow—or they could stage a skit of the cherry tree incident. March could march. April could play April fool jokes. May could do a maypole dance or crown the Queen of the May. June could have a wedding. July could celebrate the Fourth. August could "go swimming." September could have opening day at school. October could do Halloween pranks or tell a ghost story. November could pantomime a football game. December could sing Christmas carols.

What's My Name?—This mixer encourages a lot of laughter. As the guests arrive, tape the name of a famous person—movie star, television personality, cartoon character, or former President—on each person's back. Divide into pairs. Each person is to look at the name taped to the back of his or her partner. Then they ask each other only yes or no questions to find out who they are. When both have guessed their identities, they sit down.

4

FUN WITH GAMES
FOR SMALL GROUPS

People enjoy playing together. It helps break down barriers—people get to know one another better through play. It establishes rapport—people become closer friends as they laugh together. It lessens defense mechanisms—people become less defensive when they feel they are accepted by others.

Games are vitally important, and the games that follow will help you accomplish those goals you desire to achieve. But remember, most important is that everyone has fun.

MIND-READING GAMES

C-a-r—One player goes out of the room. The leader asks that someone touch any one of three articles in a row, announcing that the player who left the room can tell which one was touched. The leader calls, "Come on back," and the confederate makes a few mysterious passes over the three articles and then selects the first. That happens to be correct. The clue comes in the leader's manner of calling the mind reader back. If the leader uses a word beginning with the letter *C* the confederate knows it is the first article—"Come back." If the leader uses the letter *A* the accomplice knows it is the second—"All right." If the letter *R,* it is the third—"Ready?" To make it more confusing the confederates may decide that the first item is any consonant up to *L;* the second is any vowel; the third is any consonant from *M* to the end of the alphabet.

Variation: **Five-in-a-row**—Five books or articles. Some-one touches one of the articles. The mind reader returns. The leader points to one of the books and says, "Is it this one?" "No," answers the mind reader, "it is that one," pointing to the article touched. The clue is given in this fashion: If the leader touches the upper left-hand corner of any one of the five articles, the mind reader knows the first is the correct one; the upper right-hand corner means the second; lower left, the third; lower right, the fourth; center, the fifth.

Nine Squares—The confederate leaves the room. Mark nine squares on the ground, blackboard, or floor; or use nine articles, in rows of three each. A player indicates one of the squares. The player who has been out of the room returns and tells when the chosen square is touched by the leader. The secret is that all the squares are numbered in the minds of the leader and the confederate. The leader is careful to touch the chosen square only in its regular turn. Thus if square 3 (upper right corner) is chosen, the leader must touch 3 on the third time and must be careful not to touch square 1 or 2 in its regular order. Thus, the leader begins at the lower right, 9, saying, "Is it this one?" "No," says the confederate. The leader touches the center square, 5. "Is it this one?" "No." Now on the next turn the leader touches the upper right corner square, 3. "Is it this one?" "Yes," answers the mind reader correctly. If a square in the bottom row is selected, the leader and confederate may have some signal for indicating that the numbering, 1, 2, 3, begins at the bottom, in order to avoid touching almost every square before coming to the correct one. For instance, it may be understood that whenever the leader begins by tapping or rubbing the pencil or pointer against a leg or arm, it is the signal that the numbering has been changed and that the square touched is in the bottom row. The numbering is always done from left to right.

Sky Writing—The leader is the accomplice of one player, who leaves the group. The rest select a verb to be acted out: sing, speak, dance, snore, bat, pitch, hop, jump, or race. The player is called back. The leader pretends to write the word in the air in a mysterious chirography. Occasionally he or she claps the hands and speaks. When the leader is through, the player acts out the word. The tips are contained in what the leader says and in the hand-clapping. The first consonant in a sentence indicates the consonant the leader is conveying to the accomplice. The vowels are indicated as follows: 1 clap for A; 2 claps for E; 3 claps for I; 4 claps for O; 5 claps for U. Suppose the word is snore. The leader makes mysterious passes in the air—"See if you can follow me." There is the S. "Now do you see?" There is the N. Claps sharply 4 times. That is the O. "Rather easy, isn't it?" That gives the accomplice the R. Two claps for E. The accomplice snores.

Hands over Head—The crowd sits in a circle. One person (the accomplice) leaves the room. The leader announces that that person will be able to tell over whose head the leader will hold his or her hands. The leader moves around the circle, beginning anywhere. "Hands over head," shouts the leader, extending hands over some player's head. "Hands over head," repeats the person outside. The leader continues around the circle, stopping occasionally to extend hands over some player's head. Finally, the leader stops in front of one player, extends his or her hands and shouts, "Hands over head and rest upon," whereupon the person outside responds, "Hands over head and rest upon Sue Jenkins."

The secret: The leader, on the call, places his or her hands over the head of the person who was sitting third to the right of the leader when the accomplice left the room. The second time, it can be the person third to the left. Or it can be the tenth to the right or left. Or it can be the person before whom the leader was standing when the accomplice left the room. Or it can be the last person to speak before the accomplice left the room. The leader and accomplice should have a clear understanding of the nature and order of the clues.

Variation: **Spirits Move**—The leader extends his or her hands and says, "Spirits move." The accomplice outside answers, "Let them move." Finally the leader says, "Spirits move and rest upon ———." The accomplice outside finishes the sentence by adding the name of the person over whose head the leader's hands are extended.

GUESSING GAMES

Electric Shock—The players stand or sit in a circle. One player is It and stands inside the circle trying to discover where the electric shock is. The players hold hands and one player is designated to start the shock going. He squeezes the hand of a player either to the left or to the right. That player passes it on. The shock may move in either direction, and at any time, a player may send it back the other way. "It" watches the faces and hands of the players, trying to detect the position of the shock. When he or she guesses correctly, the player responsible becomes It.

Ring on a String—Players form a circle holding a long string tied together at the ends. They pass their hands back and forth on the string, passing a ring from one player to another. "It," in the center, tries to guess who has the ring. "It" may stop the passing at any time to make a player open his or her hands. If the player has the ring that player becomes It.

Variations: (a) **Spool on a String**—Instead of a ring use a small spool.

(b) **Lifesaver on a String**—Use a Lifesaver in the same manner.

Who's the Leader?—Players stand in a circle. One player goes out. A leader is appointed. The whole group starts clapping and continues until the player sent out returns and takes the center of the ring. "It" must discover who is leading the crowd in its actions. The leader changes from clapping, for instance, to patting the head, twirling the thumbs, jumping up and down, etc. The whole crowd does the same thing immediately. Players should not keep their eyes on the leader. It's amazing how quickly the action goes around the circle and how difficult it sometimes is to discover the leader. When finally discovered, the leader becomes It, goes out, and a new leader is selected. A good game to give the timid a chance to develop initiative. It adds to the fun if the game is played to music.

Ghost Guess—Divide guests into two groups. One group goes out of the room and sends back one person wearing a sheet that covers him or her completely. The other side tries to guess who it is. Only one guess is allowed. As soon as a name is called, the ghost throws off the sheet and discloses his or her identity. If the guess was correct, the guessing side scores one point. If incorrect, the performing side scores. Now the other group goes out and sends back a ghost. The ghost may stoop, use something to appear taller, put on shoes belonging to another person, or anything that is likely to throw the opponents off the trail.

The Guessing Game—Players are seated in a circle. One player is blindfolded and turned around 3 times. During this procedure the other players may change seats. The blindfolded player walks forward and touches someone in the circle, saying, "Can you guess?" The player touched must repeat this question 3 times, endeavoring to disguise the voice. Should the guessing player succeed, the person discovered becomes It. Otherwise, It continues until successful.

Detectives—Two or three persons go out of the room. The remaining players select some object they want the detectives to discover. It may be a button on the clothing of a certain person, a vase on a table, or anything in the room. The detectives come back and begin quizzing the individuals in the group. They cannot ask a player if he or she has the object, though they may ask someone else if a certain player has the object. The detectives are allowed to ask only three questions of any one person. By clever questioning they will soon discover the secret object. It is a good idea to discover the location first.

Who Am I?—"Who am I?" asks one of the players. "Are you dead?" "Yes." "Are you a man?" "Yes." "Are you a political figure?" "Are you in the United States?" etc. Finally some player guesses that the person is Abraham Lincoln, perhaps. The player who guesses correctly calls out, "Who am I?" and the game continues. Persons dead or alive, historic figures, characters in fiction, drama, or present-day personages may be used.

What Is It?—One player goes out of the room. The others select some item. The player returns and tries to discover the item by questioning. Only 20 questions are allowed, and only Yes and No answers. "Is it in this room?" "Is it in this town?" "Is it human?" "Is it inanimate?" If the player names the item, another player goes out and the game continues. If the answer is wrong, the player proceeds to question until 20 have been asked. This is a great game for a mentally alert group and is sometimes called **Twenty Questions**.

Percolate—One player leaves the room. The others decide on a word denoting some action, such as *walking*. The player who is It endeavors to discover the word by asking questions. The players are permitted to answer only Yes or No. "It" may ask any player as many questions as he desires, or he may be limited to three questions per person. "Do you percolate?" "Do you percolate in the evening?" "Do you percolate with your hands?" A clever questioner will soon locate the action selected.

Murder—Each player is given a slip of paper which is not to be shown to others. The players throw the slips away after reading them. Only two slips have anything on them. One reads, Murderer, and the other, District Attorney. The District Attorney leaves the room. The lights are turned out and the crowd mills around in the center of the floor. Finally the murderer puts his or her hands on someone's throat: that person screams and falls to the floor. The lights are turned on and the District Attorney takes charge. All players must answer truthfully any question put to them by the District Attorney, except the Murderer, who is privileged to lie. The District Attorney tries to discover the Murderer. Everything depends on the cleverness of the District Attorney in cross-examining witnesses. Sometimes it is advisable to select the District Attorney arbitrarily, not depending on chance.

I Have an Idea—The crowd decides on some article in the room in the absence of the person who is It. When It returns, one player says, "I have an idea." "What is it like?" asks It. "It's like you," is the answer. "Why?" "Because it shines." Another player chimes in, "I have an idea." "What is it like?" "It's like you." "Why?" "Because it stays out all night." Perhaps that will give It a clue to the article: "It is the lamp."

I Am Very, Very Tall—One player shuts his or her eyes. The other says, "I am very, very tall, I am very, very small; sometimes I'm tall; sometimes I'm small. Guess what I am now," and then either stands or stoops. The player with closed eyes must guess whether the other is tall (standing) or small (stooping). Game continues until player guesses correctly. Then the other player does the guessing. When played by a group, It stands in the center and the whole circle stands or stoops. When It guesses correctly he or she may choose someone else to be It.

Crambo—Form two groups. One goes out while the other selects a word that can be acted out, such as "trial." The members of the first group are called back and told that the word they are to guess rhymes with "mile." After conferring among themselves, they make a list of the words they think might be the correct one, and decide in what order to present them. If they have listed "smile," "style," and "trial," they first all smile broadly to enact "smile." Then they put on a "style" show. Finally they try a court scene, and the other side applauds, for it's clear that they have guessed "trial." The number of guesses is counted and the other side then goes out to try its hand at guessing and acting out the answer.

Secret Word—Guests are divided into groups of four or five. Each group selects a word with as many letters as there are persons in the group. Each player takes a letter in the word and, in turn, acts out some word beginning with that letter. For instance, if SLOW were the word, one player might act out Sleepy (yawning and stretching), another Lying (either lying down or telling a whopper), another Open (opening a book or box or door), and the fourth Washing (washing hands and face, or clothes). The other groups try to guess the secret word.

Blind Man's Bluff—A blindfolded player holding a wand stands in the center of a circle of players. The circle, hand-in-hand, moves around singing some song such as "She'll Be Comin' 'Round the Mountain." When one verse is finished, they stand still. The blindfolded player now points the wand at the circle. The player to whom it points must take hold of it and repeat three sounds indicated by the blindfolded player: crow like a rooster, meow like a cat, bark like a dog, call hogs, laugh out loud, sneeze, or cry like a baby. The performer may make every effort to disguise the voice. The blindfolded player tries to identify the noisemaker. If successful, they exchange places.

How Do You Like It?—One player goes out of the room. The others decide on some one thing. The player then returns and has the privilege of asking any player three questions, which must be answered truthfully. How do you like it? Where do you like it? When do you like it? In this way the player tries to get information that will help determine what the group has in mind.

Guessing—Numbered displays to illustrate some of these questions may be arranged, to activate the guessing. Give the guests slips on which to write their guesses. Closest guess wins.

How many beans in a quart measure?
How many peanuts in a quart jar?
How many seeds in a cup?
How many grains of corn in a glass?
How many matches in a box?

What is the diameter of a silver dollar?
What are the measurements of a dollar bill?
How many seeds in a grapefruit? An apple?
How many stars in the United States flag?
What is the weight of an egg?
How many letters are in the dictionary? (This one is
   catchy: There are just 26 letters in the dictionary.)

GAMES FOR A TRIP

Finish the Alphabet—The object of this game is to complete the alphabet by picking the letters in sequence from the signboards along the way. The game is played in two ways. One player takes the signs on one side of the road, the other takes those on the other side. The letters are called as the player sees them. The second way to play allows all players to use both sides of the road. The first player to call a letter from a particular word is the only player who can use that letter from that word. Any other player is privileged to call another letter from the same word, however. Thus one player calls "Quaker—A." Another may call "Quaker—E," if E is the letter needed. The player finishing the alphabet first wins.

Variation: The players may decide to spell a certain word. Short words may be used first—cat, dog, cow. The names of people, cities, rivers may be used.

Burying White Horses—The car is divided into two sides. The players on each side count white horses on their side. If a cemetery is passed and a player on the opposite side sees it and calls it first, the opponents must bury all the horses they have counted and start all over again. Thus if a player on the right sees a cemetery on the left, and calls it, the left side's score is canceled. The left side may prevent such a catastrophe by seeing the cemetery first and calling, "Cemetery! Alley Oop!"

Variations: (a) The cemetery idea may be eliminated. The first player to reach 25 or 50 or any agreed number is winner.

(b) Count jersey cows or any kind of cows.

(c) Count beards and mustaches.

(d) Count mailboxes. A mailbox counts one. A post office counts five.

Alliterative Travelers—The leader announces that everyone is going on a trip. They can go any place they choose, but when they tell what they are going to do there, they may use only words beginning with the initial letter of the place to which they are going. The leader then says to some player, "Traveler, where are you going?" This person answers, "California." What are you going to do there?" "Can corn, carrots, cucumbers." Or the answer could be, "Court cinema contract." If the answer is "Boston," the player might answer, "Bake beans," or "Borrow baloney."

Calling All Cities—The first player calls the name of a city. "Two" must call a city whose name begins with the last letter of the city just given. Thus if the first player calls New York, Two immediately calls Kalamazoo. Three calls Orlando. Then come Oklahoma City, Yonkers, Syracuse, Evanston, New Orleans, Seattle, El Paso, Omaha, Augusta, Akron, Newport, and so on. A player must name a city before the count of 10. Names used may not be repeated during the round. The person wins who stays in the longest. This game may be played by sides.

Buzz—One player starts the game by saying, "1." The others, in turn, say, "2," "3," "4," "5," "6." But when 7 is reached, that player must say, "Buzz." The counting goes on, but each time there is a multiple of seven or any number with seven in it, the player must substitute Buzz for the number. Thus 14, 21, 28, and others that are multiples; 17, 27, 37, and others containing the number 7 must not be said. Buzz is said instead. Penalty for infraction of this rule is dropping out of the game or paying a forfeit.

Variations: (a) Players may specify the Buzz number, making it 3, or 5, or 8.

(b) Insert the word Fizz for 5, every number that has a 5, or is a multiple of five. Keep the Buzz sequence going at the same time—1, 2, 3, 4, Fizz, 6, Buzz, 8, etc.

(c) Rather than dropping out, the player who causes the infraction starts the game over with "1."

(d) Teams can compete by seeing who can reach 50 first without a mistake.

GAMES FOR TWO (OR MORE)

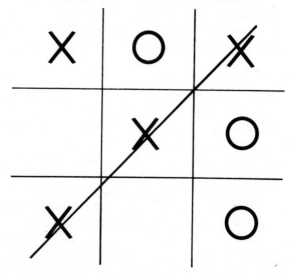

Tit-tat-toe—Two players. Each tries to get three marks in a row. Players take turns marking. One uses an X, the other an O. In this example, X got three in a row and wins. This may be a team game by using a blackboard.

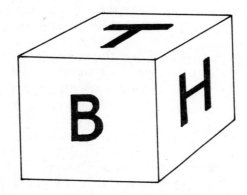

Bug—Make paper hexagon-shaped cubes with the letters B, H, T, E, L, F on the six sides. Supply pencil and paper for each player. A player throws the cubes. If B comes up the player draws the body of the bug and throws again. If an E comes up this time the player must pass, for there is no head on which to place the eye. The best second throw, therefore, is an H for the head. T is for tail, L for leg, and F for feeler. The bug must have two eyes, two feelers, and six legs in addition to its body, tail, and head before it is a complete bug. When a player tosses something he or she already has drawn, that turn is lost. A player cannot start drawing until he or she gets a B for body.

Variation: **Progressive Bug Party**—the guests play with partners. A player gets whatever the partner throws. Players may continue to play until one couple at the head table scores a complete bug, in which event they immediately ring a bell. At this signal all players stop immediately. Winners at each table progress.

Number Guessing—This is a good game for two. Guests may be paired off in order to play. Each player makes a diagram like the example.

1
22
333
4444
55555
666666
7777777
88888888
999999999

Player One holds the other hand before the writing hand, so that the opponent cannot see what number is being written. Player Two watches closely the movement of the writer's hand and pencil, and then tries to guess what number has been written. If the guess is correct, Two marks that number off his or her diagram. If Two misses, One marks the number off his or her own diagram and takes another turn. This continues until one player has no numbers left. Only one digit may be written at a time; therefore only one may be marked off at a time. Thus if player One writes 9, and player Two guesses 4, One does not mark off the whole row of 9s, but only one 9.

Fox and Geese—Seventeen geese, represented by checkers, marbles, pebbles, pegs, or cardboard counters, try to pen a fox, represented by a counter that is distinguished from the geese by color, size, material. The field consists of 33 spots or holes, marked on sheets of paper or on cardboard, or made in a wooden base or in the ground, thus:

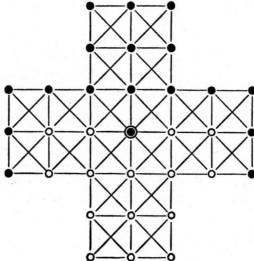

For Small Groups

Place the fox in the center. The geese are placed at every point in the three top rows and at the end of the fourth and fifth rows. One player moves the fox, while the other maneuvers the geese.

The fox has the first move. It tries to maneuver so as to jump the geese, as in checkers, and thus capture them. The fox can jump backward, forward, up, down, and across. The geese cannot jump, but may move in any direction, one space at a time. The fox is not forced to jump, but jumps only when it desires to do so. However, each player must make a move each time. The geese try to pen the fox so that it cannot move.

Making Squares—This is a good game for 2 people. Mark 5 or more rows of dots on a piece of paper. Players take turns connecting any 2 dots with a straight line—diagonals are not permitted. A player who finishes a square places his or her initial inside. When all dots have been connected, the score is indicated by the number of squares bearing a player's initials.

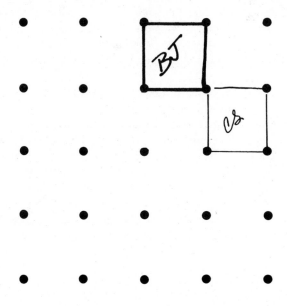

Stone, Paper, Scissors (originally a Japanese game)—
Players line up in two rows facing one another. One pair of
opponents advance with hands behind them. The leader
counts, "One-two-three." On "three," the two players bring
their hands forward in the position they choose, according
to whether they decide to be stone, paper, or scissors. The
stone is represented by clenched fists; the paper by open
hands, palms down; the scissors by extending the index
and middle fingers. Stone beats scissors because it dulls
them. Scissors beat paper because they can cut it. Paper
beats stone because it can cover it. Points are counted as
the opponents contest.

Variations: (a) All players advance to middle and face
opponents. At "three" all players bring forth hands to
represent stone, paper, or scissors.

(b) All players advance, and at "three," put forth hands,
but this time all players on a side represent the same thing.
A mistake by any player disqualifies the team and scores a
point for the other side. Therefore the players must get
together to decide what they will represent. The first side
to make ten points in this manner wins.

(c) Koreans play a variation in which they represent
Man, Gun, and Tiger. The man is represented by holding
fingers up to represent long, flowing mustaches; the gun by
aiming index finger; the tiger by growling and holding
claws out.

(d) The Japanese have a relay race built on this game.
The course is square or rectangular in shape. It can be
marked off by stones, sticks, or trees at the four corners.
Runners line up at opposite corners at the same end of the
field. At a signal, the first player on each team starts to run
around the square. When the two runners meet, they put
their hands behind them and say, "Jan-Kem-Po." On "Po"
they hold out their hands, representing either stone,
paper, or scissors. The winner continues. The loser drops
out and a new player starts out from that side to meet the

opposing runner. Each time two runners meet, they stop and do Jan-Kem-Po, the winner always proceeding. The first team to get a runner to the opponent's corner wins.

Odd or Even—This ancient game can be traced back to early Greece and Rome. It is a familiar game in Europe.

A small number of beans or other counters is held in the hand, fist closed. "Odd or even?" says the holder. If the opponent guesses "Even," and the number held is odd, the holder claims a counter from the opponent, saying, "Give me one to make it even." The game continues until one of the players is out of counters.

The game can easily be adapted for sides, each time a different player representing his side.

Marble Golf (Knucks)—Three or more holes 4″ to 5″ in diameter, are dug in the ground, about 8′ or 10′ apart. They may, or may not be in a straight line, as desired.

The starting line is 5′ or 6′ from the first hole. One player starts by "knuckling down" at the starting line and shooting at Hole 1. If that player's marble goes into Hole 1, he or she plays for Hole 2, and so on, back to Hole 1. If the marble fails to go into any hole, the next player starts. If a player hits an opponent's marble, the player gets an extra shot. If a player holes a marble and another player's marble is near the rim of the hole ready to go in at the next shot, the opponent's marble may be hit, driving it away, before proceeding to the next hole. Some players acquire great skill in playing an opponent's marble, so that they can use it for several consecutive shots. In playing out of a hole, players must knuckle with the hand at the rim of the hole from which the play is made, or they may be allowed one hand's span from the rim.

The last player out must hold the fist clenched, knuckles up, at the rim of Hole 1 while each of the other players, in turn, plumps a marble, trying to hit the knuckles. Three shots are allowed at the knuckles.

Mumblety-peg—This ancient game is played on dirt or soft turf. A pocketknife is used. The knife must stick in the earth, being thrown from various successive positions, as follows: (1) The knife, small blade open, is held in the palm, first of the right and then of the left hand, point up toward the thumb. The player brings the hand up and over, turning it so that the back of the hand is toward the body, with thumb and knife point down.

(2) The knife rests successively on the right and left fists, point upward, and thrown sideways.

(3) The point is pressed against each finger and thumb in succession, and cast outward.

(4) Held by the point and flipped from the breast, nose, cheeks, eyes, and forehead.

(5) From each ear, arms crossed, and taking hold of opposite ear with the free hand.

(6) Over the head backward.

(7) Held point downward and dropped through circle made by thumb and forefinger of free hand.

(8) Tossed into the air, tipping the handle up with the finger to give it an end-over-end motion.

(9) Putting free hand down as a barrier and placing the knife at a slant, point touching the turf, flip knife over barrier to opposite side.

(10) Blade between the first and second fingers of one hand while the handle is between the same fingers on the other hand. Flip blade over.

(11) Point of blade held between forefinger and thumb. With a sweeping motion the player hits the turf with his hand, releasing the knife as he does it.

If the knife does not stick, the next player takes a turn. The first to conclude the series wins. The winner gets to drive a wooden matchstick into the ground with six blows of the knife handle—three with eyes shut and three with eyes open. The loser must extract the peg from the earth with the teeth.

"ARTISTIC" GAMES

Dressing Lollipops—Provide each guest with a lollipop. Have several work tables and materials available—crepe paper, crayons, paper, paste, scissors. Each person is to dress a lollipop, making features to represent various types of characters—the handle-bar mustache villain, Goldilocks, Red Riding Hood, etc.

Allow five to ten minutes and then put the lollipops on display. After the display the guests can form groups and put on some brief puppet shows with their dolls.

Fashion Show—Guests are paired off. Newspapers, crepe paper, pins, library paste, scissors, and style designs are made available. Partners dress in whatever style appeals. There are all sorts of possibilities—bridal costume, peasant outfit, dress of the future, colonial style. When the costumes have been finished, climax this event with a fashion show.

Cooperative Art—Each player draws a head and neck, not allowing any others to see what he or she has drawn. The player then folds the paper once and passes it to another player, who draws the body. Again the paper is folded so what has been drawn cannot be seen, and it is passed to the next player, who draws the legs and feet. No player allows others to see what has been drawn. After the "work of art" has been finished the paper is unfolded and the "marvelous" creation is put on display.

Rapid-fire Artists—Divide into groups and supply paper, pencils, crayons, etc. Each group sends an "artist" to the leader. The leader whispers to each artist some animal or other thing to draw. The artists rush back to their respective groups and begin to draw furiously. As soon as an artist's group recognizes the object being drawn, the members shout out its name. The artist must not give any tip other than the drawing. Each time, a new "artist" must be sent to the leader.

Variation: **Draw That Tune**—The leader whispers the name of a popular song. The artists return to their drawing boards and illustrate the tune.

Paper Plate Art—Each guest is given a paper plate or a piece of cardboard. On the table are pencils, several sets of colored crayons, marking pens, etc. Each person is asked to illustrate some nursery rhyme, song, book title, or other given subject. One group used this idea at a banquet. Since it was a Tree Banquet, everyone was asked to draw a scene that contained trees. There were some really lovely creations.

Make a Balloon Face—With construction paper, yarn, felt-tip markers, tape, and any other supply you might envision, each person or group designs a face on a balloon. Judges select the winner.

OTHER GOOD SMALL-GROUP GAMES

Flying Feather—Form groups of not more than 10. Players join hands and try to keep a downy feather up in the air by blowing. A leader or one of the group may toss the feather into the air. Often players can keep the feather up for a long time. Players must not break hands. If there are several groups, the one that keeps its feather up longest wins. In this case the feather would be tossed into the air at a signal from the leader.

Variation: Music may be played and players move in rhythm as they endeavor to keep the feather flying. Light-weight balloons may also be used.

Grocery Store—Players form two lines. One player from each side steps forward and the leader calls out a letter. The player who first calls the name of some grocery article beginning with that letter scores a point for that side. Prompting from the sidelines subtracts a point for each infraction.

Numbered Chairs—Players are seated in one row of chairs and numbered off. The chairs retain the same numbers throughout, though the players may change. Player Number One calls "Five." Immediately, Five must respond with another number. When a player whose number is called does not respond immediately that player goes to the foot of the row. All players below that chair move up one space and change their numbers by doing so. Thus Six becomes Five, and so on down the line. Numbers are called rapidly and special effort is made to send the top players to the foot.

Birds Have Feathers—The players flap their arms flying fashion when the leader names something with feathers. If a player flaps his wings on the calling of something that does not have feathers, that player drops out. The leader may flap his or her own "wings" at any time to confuse the others. The calls are made rapidly. "Birds have feathers. Geese have feathers. Ducks have feathers. Frogs have feathers. Goats have feathers. Swans have feathers."

The Queen's Headache—A blindfolded player is seated at one end of the room, with 3 empty chairs on either side. It is announced that the queen has a headache and doesn't want to be disturbed. Players are to try to walk up to the empty chairs without disturbing the queen, as the queen will groan as soon as she hears footsteps approaching and the players who are walking must sit down wherever they are. Keep up the game until six players have succeeded in getting to the empty chairs, or until interest wanes.

Variation: Players are seated in a circle, with the queen seated at the center. Players try to cross to the opposite side. Any player may cross and demand any seat, and the player in that seat must move to another. Whenever the queen groans, players standing must sit on the floor until the queen stops groaning.

Beast, Bird, or Fish—The players stand or sit in a circle. One player in the center has a beanbag or ball, tosses this to a player in the circle, and says quickly, "Beast, bird, or fish! Beast!" The player to whom the bean bag has been thrown must answer immediately with the name of a beast: Fox, Dog, or Mule. If the center player counts to 10 before a proper response is made, the player becomes It.

Variation: Instead of throwing an object, the center player may simply point a finger.

Mute Spelling—Players indicate vowels by signs. Right hand raised means A; left hand raised means E; pointing to eye means I; puckering lips as if to say "O" means O; pointing to someone means U. Players line up on 2 sides. Leader calls word to be spelled and indicates a player to spell. The player must say all the consonants but be mute on the vowels, only giving the proper sign. Thus: C—raise right hand—T, in answer to "cat" called by the leader. Other letters may be added to the mute list—whistle for R, hiss for S, shade eyes for C, stutter for K, "humph" for H, growl for G.

What Is My Thought Like?—One player announces that he or she has a thought in mind that will be disclosed later.

Each player, in turn, must tell what the thought is like. "It is like a piano," says one. "It is like a hot potato," says another. "It is like the deep blue sea," says still another. The leader writes down each answer.

After the last player has answered, the leader announces that he or she is thinking, for instance, of a baseball game. Now each player, in turn must tell why the leader's thought is like that player's analogy. "It is like a piano because the pitch is important." "It is like a hot potato because the hotter it is, the harder it is to handle." "It is like the deep blue sea because sometimes it is pretty rough." So each player must have an answer. Sometimes tall stretching has to be done to bear out the analogy. There will be some side-splitting analogies.

Trust Walk—Participants line up in two equal teams, facing one another. Members of one team close their eyes and do not open them under any circumstances. Each member of the other team selects someone from the closed-eyes team and guides that person around for a period of 5 to 10 minutes. No one is to talk. The players with closed eyes are to trust their partners completely. No foul play or risky manuever is permitted. After a period of time, the players may open their eyes and share with their partners their feeling and emotions. Then reverse the procedure.

5

FUN WITH ACTIVE GAMES

Active games can be played indoors or outdoors, depending upon the occasion. Remember to alternate active with inactive games, so as not to tire your players. Be aware of the age group when playing active games. Many are not suitable for small children or older adults. Be wise in your selection.

GAMES WITH BALLOONS

Balloons can offer many hours of fun and pleasure. They can be used in camp settings as well as at indoor parties.

Balloon Toss—See who can toss an inflated balloon farther. As each balloon is tossed, mark the spot where it first touches down. The person who tosses it the greatest distance wins.

Balloon Stomp—Tie an inflated balloon on the leg of each participant, about 6 inches above the ankle. At a signal, participants are to try to burst other players' balloons by stepping on them. When a balloon bursts, that player is out of the game. The last player with a still-inflated balloon is the winner.

Variation: Tie balloons on both ankles.

Balloon Chopsticks Relay—Each team will need a pair of 18″ to 24″ dowel rods to serve as chopsticks. A balloon is placed between the chopsticks, near the end (not in the middle). Player One is to carry the balloon between the chopsticks around an object (chair, post, trash can, etc.) and back to the next player. Player Two takes the chopsticks and the balloon from Player One and repeats the run. Should the balloon fall, it is not to be touched with the hands. It must be picked up with the chopsticks.

Balloon Sit—Each participant is given a balloon to inflate. Players line up in teams. On the signal, one player from each team runs to a chair (a chair for each team is placed about 30′ from the starting line), sits on the balloon until it bursts, and returns to the starting position. The first team to finish is the winner.

Spank a Balloon—Players tie inflated balloons to the back of their belts. The balloons should hang the proper length down their backs. Give each player a folded or rolled-up newspaper. The object is to see who can swat the other players' balloons until they burst. When a balloon bursts, that player is out of the game. The person who is left with balloon still inflated is the winner.

Balloon Basketball—With about 6 to 10 players to a team, 2 teams sit in facing chairs, in rows about 2′ apart. Each team has a goalie. These players sit, one at each end of the "court," facing each other, with arms held in a circle like a basketball goal. There is a referee for each team. A referee tosses a large inflated balloon into the space between the two teams. Players begin to swat the balloon toward their opponents' goal. The balloon is to be swatted, not tossed, into a goalie's arms. Should the balloon go out of bounds, the referees toss it back into the center of the group. Players are to remain in their chairs and should never stand to reach the balloon. Goals count 2 points. A timekeeper should allow about 3 minutes for each quarter. The referees' decisions are final.

Balloon Volleyball—If the day is windy, it is best to play this game inside. The net can be a regular volleyball net or a makeshift net (cord, sheet, table, etc.). The court should be in proportion to the playing area. If inside, a net should be 3 to 4' high. Usual volleyball rules apply. Players can stand or sit on the floor. On a calm day outside or in a gymnasium, use a weather balloon. Serve and hit the balloon with the head only.

Hug a Balloon—Partners place a large balloon, fully inflated, between them and hug each other until the balloon bursts. This can be a contest between couples.

Balloon Stuffing—Members of each team wear sweat suits or long underwear. They blow up balloons and stuff them in their clothing. At the end of a given period, count the number of balloons by popping them with a pin. The team with the most balloons stuffed wins.

Balloon Between the Knees—Each relay team has one medium-sized inflated balloon. The first players in line place the balloons between their knees, then walk, hop, or scoot along to an object (chair, ball, etc.), around it, and back to the starting position. They hand the balloons to the next team members. Should the balloon be dropped, the players pick it up and continue the relay. The players cannot carry the balloon in their hands.

Balloon Blow-up—Each contestant blows up a medium to large balloon until it bursts.

Water-Balloon Football—Fill small to medium-sized balloons with water and place in a container near the playing field. There are 11 members on each team, just as in touch football. One team kicks off by tossing a water balloon to the opposing side. Should the balloon burst when received, the first team has a first down. Should an opposing team member catch the still-filled balloon, that player runs the ball back toward the first team's goal. To stop the player, the balloon must be burst. Use a new balloon for each play. Passes can be thrown. If a player catches a pass and the balloon bursts, the down begins at the point where the balloon burst. No tackles are allowed. Ground rules should be decided before play begins.

Water-Balloon Over-and-Under Relay—Each team lines up single file, an arm's length apart. The first player on each team has a filled water balloon. At a signal, they pass the balloons over their heads to the next players, who pass the balloons between their legs to the players behind them. This process continues until the last players receive the balloons. They then run to the front of the lines and begin the process over again. When the first players return to the starting position, the game is over. Each player must do the opposite action from the player before.

Water-Balloon Toss—Two players stand facing each other, an arm's length apart. One player hands the other a filled water balloon. Each player takes a step backward. The balloon is then gently tossed back to the first player. Each player takes another step backward. This process goes on until the balloon bursts. The balloon should be tossed underhanded.

Balloon Goal—At each corner of the room, strings are stretched at a height of 6 or 7'. The leader tosses two balloons of different colors into the air at the center of the floor. One team is Green (if you have a green balloon) and the other is Yellow (if you have a yellow balloon). Each team tries to get its balloon over either of two goals in diagonal corners of the room. A point is scored each time this is done. There is no pause in play, the balloon being immediately put into play again by the leader at the center of the floor. Players may play anywhere on the floor after the balloons are put in play.

Balloon Race—Players are equipped with ping-pong paddles and inflated balloons. They bat the balloons to an agreed goal and back to the starting line. Balloons must be batted through the air. If one falls to the ground the player must pick it up and bat it into the air again.

Variations: (a) Use fans instead of paddles.

(b) Use brooms and propel the balloons along the floor or ground.

Balloon Battle Royal—Form partners. One partner has a toy balloon tied to the left ankle, the string being at least a yard long. Partners must keep arms linked all during the battle, the player with the balloon on the right. They try to protect their balloon, at the same time trying to step on and burst all the others. This continues until only one team survives, if and when they do.

Air Balloon Relay—Each team of four members is given a small inflated balloon. All balloons are tossed into the air at a given signal. Members of a team blow on their balloon to keep it in the air as they all walk together to and around an object and back to the starting line. Should the balloon fall, a player picks it up and tosses it back into the air.

103

BEANBAG GAMES

Beanbag Baseball—The field is marked off in nine 1′ squares. The top squares are marked Ball, Second, Foul; the second row, Strike, Home Run, Strike; the bottom squares, First, Out, Third. Batters stand about 10 feet away and try to throw the beanbag onto a square that will put them on base. Batters continue to throw until they make a base or an out. A beanbag touching a line is a strike. When a batter gets on base he or she takes a position back of the base secured, not stepping on the square. Runners advance only when they are forced by the next batter.

Variation: **Washer Baseball**—use washers instead of beanbags and reduce size of squares to 6″.

Garden Gate—Two lines of players face each other, 6′ apart. A leader for each line stands beside a bucket. These 2 leaders stand 4′ apart. They are the posts of the "gate." Each player has a bean bag.

At the starting signal both team's first players (the ones nearest the leaders) run down inside their lines, around their end players, back up behind their lines and back through the gate, dropping their beanbags in their buckets as they pass, and go back to position. As soon as Number One passes Number Two, that player follows. And so each in turn runs around the line and through the "garden gate."

Five points are awarded to the first team to have all players back in position. One point is taken off for each beanbag that lands outside the bucket.

Rabbit and Dog—Players stand in a circle. Two beanbags of different colors are used, one to represent the rabbit and the other the dog. One player receives the rabbit and a player on the opposite side of the circle receives the dog. When the signal is given to start, the rabbit and the dog are passed from player to player. The dog chases the rabbit. The players help the rabbit to get away and the dog to catch the rabbit. If the rabbit completes three rounds of the circle without being caught, it is safe.

Center Pitch—Players pitch beanbags into a heavy wastebasket or bucket set a good distance away from players. Teams should have different colored beanbags. One beanbag to a player. Members of one team all line up and toss at a given signal. The other team tosses. Three to five turns for each side. The side with most beanbags in bucket wins.

200 or Bust—On the ground or floor, make a target with three circles. Form teams. Use 3 beanbags; each player gets 3 tosses. To go out, a team must make a perfect 200. If it goes over, it must start again. First side to make a perfect score wins. A line counts for the larger score.

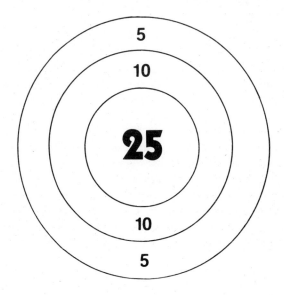

Hot Beanbags—Players form a circle. Several beanbags are distributed to the group. When the music starts, players pass beanbags to the right. When the music stops, or at some other signal, players having possession of or throwing down beanbags must drop out. As the circle grows smaller, fewer beanbags should be used, until only one is left for the last four or five players. The last player left is winner.

Beanbag Throw—Form teams with 8 to 10 players each. Each team should have the same number of beanbags. A circle 12″ to 18″ in diameter is drawn 6′ in front of each team. Teams line up single file at a starting line. At a signal, the first player on each team tosses beanbags toward the circle. For each one that lands within the circle, the team gets a point. A bag that is not completely within the circle does not count. After all the beanbags have been thrown, the player runs up to the circle, gathers all the bags, races back to the starting line, and hands them to the next player. This continues until all players have had a turn. The team with the highest score is declared the winner.

Hit the Can—A trash basket, box, or some other receptacle can be used for the goal. Players on each team line up in single file. Six lines, 1 yard apart, have been drawn on the ground between the players and the receptacle; the first line is 1 yard from the receptacle, and the last line is 6 yards from it.

The first player on each team starts at the line closest to the receptacle and tosses the beanbag from there. If the beanbag goes into the receptacle, the player moves back to the next line and tosses, and so on. When that player misses, the next player on the team moves to the first line and tosses the beanbag toward the receptacle. They do this until each player either misses or gets all six tosses into the receptacle. The team with the most successful tosses is the winner.

Hurly-Burly Beanbag—Players sit in single file by teams. The first person in line tosses the bag into the air. The second player in line claps his or her hands while the bag is in the air and then attempts to catch it. Player Two then tosses it to Player Three, and so on, until the last player has caught the beanbag. If a player misses the bag, that player just picks it up and tosses it backward to the next player. When the last player receives the beanbag, he or she hops to the starting position and begins the process all over. When Player One returns to the number one position, the game is over. The team to finish first wins.

RACES AND RELAYS

Horse and Rider Race—One player mounts the back of another, legs aound waist and arms around shoulders. In this position they race to the goal. When they reach the goal, they exchange positions and race back to the starting line.

Variation: **Mule and Rider Race**—The mule goes down on all fours. The rider mounts the mule's back and they race to the finish line.

Hurdle Race—The ten players on each team line up in single file. Players Number One and Two hold a broomstick or rope between them, at least 6″ off the ground. They run down the line of players, one on each side of the line, and their teammates jump the hurdle as it moves along. As soon as they reach the last player, Number Two returns to the head of the line and starts down again with Number Three in the same manner. Then Number Three runs with Number Four, and so on, until Number One is back at the head of the line.

Thumb Bottle Race—Fill a soft-drink bottle with water. Teams form single file lines, standing up or sitting side by side. The leader of each team begins by placing a thumb over the mouth of the filled bottle. The leader then passes the bottle to the next player (bottle must remain upside down throughout the game), and then to the next, and so on. The last to receive the bottle returns it back up line. The team with the most water left in its bottle wins.

Run Sheep Run—Form two equal sides, each with a captain. A home base is indicated. One group is the "sheep." They go out and hide. Their captain comes back when they are ready, and goes with the opposing side as it hunts for the sheep. At the opportune time, the captain yells, "Run, sheep, run!" All the sheep immediately rush for home base, as do the hunters. If the sheep beat the hunters to home base, they hide again. If not, the hunters become sheep.

Skin the Snake Race—Two or more teams, with 5 to 10 players each, stand in single file. All players stoop over, putting their right hands between their legs and grasping the left hand of the player behind. At the signal, the last person in line lies down on his or her back, putting the feet between the legs of the person standing in front. All players then walk backward, straddling the prone bodies of their teammates, each player lying down in turn. As soon as all are flat on their backs, the last person gets up and starts back, pulling the next player up, and so on, until all are in their original position. Players must not release hands.

Back-to-Back Race—Determine the goal at 25, 50, or 75 yards. Teams are divided into partners. Partners stand back to back and link arms. At the signal, one partner runs forward while the other runs backward until they reach the goal line. As soon as both touch the goal line, they start back, reversing positions. Now the one who ran backward runs forward, while the other runs backward. They have not finished until both runners touch the finish line.

Variations: (a) Tie partners together at the waist, leaving the arms free.

(b) Two sets of partners (one set facing the other) race with arms around one another's waists.

Broom-Horse Race—Each team needs a yardstick or a 3' dowel rod, a broom, and a soft-drink bottle or tin can. Players line up single file. The leaders ride their broom horses as they push the bottle or can to an object and back to the starting line. They then give the stick and horse to the next in line. The team to finish first wins.

Chinese Hop—Ten sticks are placed about one foot apart. The player must hop over these sticks without touching any of them. Touching a stick disqualifies the player. After jumping over the last stick, the player, still on one foot, must reach down and pick up the stick, then hop back over the remaining sticks. The player then drops the stick, hops over the 9, picks up the ninth stick, and returns to the starting point, again hopping the remaining sticks. This continues until all sticks have been picked up. A player is disqualified if both feet touch the ground, or if a foot touches a stick.

Variations: (a) The game may be used as a race. In this case, a player who fouls must start over.

(b) A relay may be run. The second player would put down the 10 sticks. The third would pick them up, and so on.

Leapfrog—Players stand single file. The first player bends over and grasps his or her own ankles. The next player places hands on One's back and, straddling One, leaps over. Two then assumes the same position as Number One. Number Three leaps Numbers One and Two and assumes the same position. When all players have been leaped, Number One rises and leaps over each of the others. And so it continues as long as desired. Or a definite course can be marked out. Players continue until the course is covered.

Spud Spear Relay—Each team is provided with a fork. Potatoes are placed 4' to 20' apart, depending on the space available. Player Number One on each team runs to the first potato, spears it with the fork, carries it back, drops it in a basket, and hands the fork to the next player. Number Two retrieves the second potato in the same manner. The first team to get all its potatoes in its basket wins. Hands must not touch potatoes at any time.

Partner Chair Relay—Partners link arms and run to a designated point, one carrying a folding chair. At the goal, the one partner opens the chair, sets it up, and the other partner sits down in it. That partner then gets up, the chair is folded, partners link arms and run to starting point, and chair is handed to next players. Four or five sets of partners make a team.

Circle Chair Relay—Divide into two teams of 10 or more players each. Players are seated in chairs arranged in two circles, facing out. At the signal, the leaders of the teams start around their circles. As soon as they complete the circuit and are seated the next players on each team make the circuit. First team whose players complete the round wins.

Variations: (a) Run around instead of walking.

(b) Contestants carry their chairs with them.

(c) As soon as the first runner passes the person on the

right, that player gets up and follows. The third player follows the second, and so on.

Kite String Relay—Each team has a ball of kite string. Teams line up in single file. The first player, Number One, wraps the string once around his or her waist and passes it to the next player, who does the same. This continues down the line until all players have wrapped the string around themselves. The last player unwraps the string, rolls it up, and passes it to the next player in front, who does the same. This goes back up the line until player One has unwrapped the string and rolled it back on the ball. The first team to finish wins.

Variations: (a) Use a spool of thread. Players wrap the thread around a finger 5 times before passing the spool on.

(b) Tie a piece of string to a spoon. Players drop the spoon and string down their shirts and/or pant's legs before passing it to the next in line. Then reverse until spoon and string have been removed from last pant's leg and/or shirt.

Water Pitcher Race—Each team has a pitcher full of water, an empty pitcher, and a paper cup. The empty pitcher is on a table at the starting line. The full pitcher is on a table about 40 feet from the starting line. On the signal, the first player races to the full pitcher, fills the cup with water, races back to the starting line, pours the water into the empty pitcher, and hands the cup to the next player, who repeats the action. This continues until the once empty pitcher is full. The team to fill its pitcher first wins.

Revolving Door—Players sit in about 40 straight chairs placed in a square, 10 chairs to each side. In the center of the square is an object (another chair) which must be passed by each player in turn. The players in the first chairs of each row race around the object and to the last chair in their own rows. While they are racing, each player is to move one chair to the right and thus leave the last chair vacant for the players who are circling the object. When the first players sit down, the second players race around the object while everyone shifts to the next chair. When player One returns to his or her original chair, the race is over. The first team to finish wins.

Variation: Each team leader holds a ball (or balloon or rag). On the signal, the player races around the center object, sits down in the last chair (after other players have shifted), and passes the ball down the row until the player in the first seat receives it. That player then races, passes the object down, and so on, until the first player is again in his or her original seat.

Four for Seven—This contest requires great cooperation and smart thinking. Seven participants are to go from point A to point B, with only four points of contact with the ground at a time. The distance to be covered should be about 30'. The seven players are to plan and execute a way to get from point A to point B with only four feet, legs, *or* hands touching the ground at any one time. They may not use props, and each player must be touching one of the others at all times.

Ankle Grab Race—Divide into teams. Each player grabs his or her ankles, runs from the starting line around an object and back again. First team to finish wins.

Caterpillar Race—From 4 to 8 participants are needed. The players sit one behind the other in a straight line on the ground or floor. Each player places legs around the waist and feet in the lap of the player in front. The first player is the only one allowed to place his or her feet on the ground or floor. The resulting caterpillar, using hands only, scoots from the starting line to the finish line. The entire caterpillar must cross the line. A good relay game.

Can-Can—Participants sit in a large circle, facing in. On opposite sides inside the circle, place 2 chairs for goals. Scatter 6 cans within the circle. Blindfold 2 players. Instruct them to find 3 cans apiece and to place the cans at their own goals. One player is to place the cans *on* the goal chair; the other is to place the cans *under* the goal chair. They may take a can from the opponent's goal and place it at their own goal. The cans must be placed one at a time. The first one to complete the task wins.

BALL GAMES

Straddle Ball—Players stand in a circle, feet in straddle position, touching the feet of the players on either side. "It" stands in the center of the circle with a basketball or volleyball and tries to roll the ball out of the circle between the legs of some player. That player tries to stop the ball with his or her hands and roll the ball back to It. If It does succeed in rolling the ball through some player's straddled legs, that player becomes It. "It" may fake a roll in one direction and roll in another. Much depends upon speed and surprise moves.

Guarding the Treasure—One player who is It guards the treasure (a football, soccer ball, or tin can). "It" may be called the miser while the others are robbers, or the guard, while the others are the enemy. The guard can take a position directly over the ball—the treasure—one foot on each side of it, stand directly back of it, or keep moving around it. The rest of the players circle about attempting to get the treasure by kicking it away without being tagged by the guard. If a player succeeds, another immediately kicks it, and soon the ball is being followed by the whole crowd. They do their best to keep the guard from regaining possession. No player except the guard is allowed to touch the "treasure" with the hands. If the guard succeeds in tagging any player with the ball before another kicks it, the tagged player becomes the guard.

Call Ball—Player one bounces a ball up against a wall and calls the name or number of another player, who endeavors to catch the ball on the rebound before it touches the ground again. If successful, that player bounces the ball and calls some other player. If the called player fails to make the catch, player One throws the ball again and calls another name. When thrown, the ball must hit the floor or ground first, and then the wall, so that it will come looping back.

Jump the Shot—A stuffed sack, (volleyball, or soccer ball) is tied to the end of a long heavy string or rope. The players form a circle with a radius just a little less than the length of the string. A player in the center swings the sack around just above the ground so that each player must jump to keep from being hit on the feet. Any player who is hit must take the place of the player at the center.

Variation: Use a fishing pole instead of the string and sack.

Spud—The leader bounces or tosses a soccer ball, volleyball, or tennis ball and calls the name or number of some player. That player, One, recovers the ball while all the other players scatter about the gymnasium or playing field. From the point of recovery One attempts to hit another player with the ball. Each miss counts one Spud against player One. After missing, One must recover the ball and throw again until someone is hit, except that three spuds puts a player out. When a player is hit that player must recover the ball and attempt to hit someone else.

Bottle Ball—The ideal number for this game is 5 on each side, on a playing field 60' x 30'. The 3 end players must guard 2 bottles each. These 2 bottles should be placed about 18″ apart. The throwers try to shoot a basketball (volleyball or soccer ball) through the other side, their opponents blocking the ball as best they can. Players foul when they step beyond the midway line. Score 5 points for each bottle knocked down; 10 points for each shot that goes between the 2 bottles; 1 point for each shot rolling over the line; 1 point for each shot going under a string stretched across the end of the field at the height of 6′; 1 point off for each toss going over that string without being tipped over by an opponent.

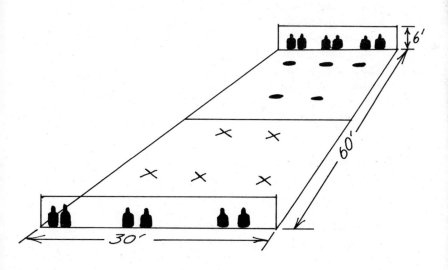

Bottle Ball

Circle Bounce—Form two circles of equal size. A leader is selected for each group and handed a game ball or volleyball. At the signal, the leader, player One, passes the ball to the person standing next to the person next to One's right. In other words, One passes the ball to player Three, who passes the ball *back* to player Two. Two passes the ball to Four, who passes the ball *back* to Three. Three in turn passes the ball to Five, who passes it *back* to Four. This continues until player One receives the ball again. The team that finishes first wins.

Variation: Bounce the ball instead of passing it.

Circle Kick Ball—Form a circle of about 10 players. Place a beach ball or rubber game ball (*not* a heavy type kickball or soccer ball), in the middle of the group. The players join hands. Players attempt to kick the ball out of the circle between other players' feet, or between 2 players' legs. Players may move around, but must not release hands. If a player releases hands, kicks the ball higher than waist height, or allows the ball to go out between his or her own feet, then that player is eliminated from the game. The game is over when only 3 players are left.

Circle Touch Ball—Players form a circle around one player. Players in the circle stand 2 or 3' apart. A basketball or soccer ball is passed here and there in the circle, while the center player tries to touch it. If successful, the player who held it at the time is It. If the ball is touched while in the air or on the ground the player who last had it is It. The players try to keep the ball away from the center player. They fake throws and try to confuse the player in other ways.

Variation: A smaller ball is used and the center player must catch the ball instead of merely touching it.

Ante Over—One team of players is stationed on one side of a small building and the other on the other side. One player on the team that has the ball shouts, "Ante Over!" as he or she tosses the ball over the building. This warns the other team to be on the lookout for the ball. They try to catch it. If the ball is not caught, any member of that team may pick it up and throw it back, calling, "Ante Over!" as the throw is made. If the ball is caught, all the members of the catcher's team run around the shed, and the player who made the catch tries to hit some player of the other team with the ball before they all get to the other side of the shed. As soon as the other team realizes that the ball has been caught, it runs for safety on the other side of the shed. A player who is hit joins the other team. Each time the ball is caught, some players on the catching team run around one way and some the other, so as to confuse the opposing side, since it doesn't know who has the ball. The game ends when all the players of one team have been caught. If this seems likely not to happen, the teams decide on a number of throws before counting players to determine the winner.

Bicycle Polo—Four players make a team. Each player is mounted on a bicycle. The game is played just like regular polo except that the players use croquet mallets, and the ball is a solid rubber ball, or any ball 6 to 10″ in diameter.

Feetball—Players sit side by side in a straight line or a circle. A ball (tennis ball, softball, or balloon) is passed from player to player, using only the feet. If the ball is dropped, it is picked up with the feet and the passing continues. The game ends when the ball reaches the end of the line or the beginning of the circle.

CONTESTS

Hand Push—Two players stand flat-footed, facing one another at arm's length. The arms are extended, palm out.

The players hold palms together, pushing or faking a push, until one player is thrown off-balance.

Hand Wrestle—Two players stand with legs spread, a stance similar to that of a dueler. They grasp right hands and each twists, turns, and shoves with the wrist, trying to throw the opponent off-balance. The feet must not be moved from position.

Indian Wrestle—Two contestants lie side by side, flat on their backs, with feet in opposite directions. Adjacent arms are locked. At the signal, adjacent legs are interlocked at the knee. The wrestler who makes the opponent roll over wins.

Rooster Fight—Hands are placed on ankles. Two players jostle one another with their shoulders, trying to throw each other off-balance or loosen each other's hold on the ankles.

All Stand Up—Two players sit back to back with arms folded. Each tries to get up by pushing against the other.
Variations: (a) Try the same contest with arms locked.
(b) Try with a large group in a line.

One-Leg Wrestle—Two players stand on one leg, clasping right hands. Each tries to make the opponent touch the free hand or the other foot to the ground. The free hand may not touch the opponent.

Brothers of the I-Will-Arise—Contestants lie flat on their backs, arms folded. At a signal, they rise to sitting position and then to their feet without using their arms. If you think this is easy, try it. It is good exercise for the abdominal muscles.

Pull Up—Two contestants sit facing each other. The knees are straight and the feet are braced against the opponent's feet. In this position each grasps one end of a stick and tries to pull the opponent forward. A contestant who bends the knees loses.

Cross-Hand Shove—Two contestants cross arms at wrist and clasp hands. In this position they try to shove each other out of a 6' circle. No tripping allowed.

Rattlesnake—Blindfold 2 players, the rattlesnake and the hunter. Give the snake a baby rattle or a medicine bottle with a few pebbles in it. The hunter gets a rolled-up newspaper or a piece of foam-rubber tubing to serve as a weapon. The players stand in a circle with the snake and the hunter in the middle. Each is turned around five times and then released. The snake is to rattle the rattlers. The hunter is to locate and hit the snake with the weapon. After the snake has been hit several times, they change positions, but this time, do not blindfold the hunter—let the hunter really hit the snake. Don't overdo it.

Trust Fall—A platform about 4 to 6' off the ground will be needed. The volunteer climbs onto the platform, stiffens back and legs, folds arms across chest, closes eyes, and slowly (without bending) falls off the platform *backward* into the arms of six teammates. The catchers are to stand with arms stretched out ready to catch their falling comrade. It is best to face each other, shoulder to shoulder, alternate arms, and be on level ground. The person falling must not bend, for the weight would be centered and chances of falling through the waiting arms heightened.

Variation: **Trust Dive**—From a platform about 3 to 4' high, participant dives into the arms of his or her teammates. The four catchers stand face to face with shoulders together, arms outstretched, palms up, farther from the platform than during the trust fall.

Dismounting Cavalry—There are 2 teams, 2 players to a team. Two are the horses, the other two the riders. The riders mount their "steeds," arms around shoulders and legs wrapped around bodies. The horses grasp the legs of their riders. The teams contest, the riders trying to pull one another from their mounts. Play the game on soft turf for hard falls are possible   he game is rough and players should wear old clothes.

Variations: (a) **Cavalry Battle Royal**—The same, except that there are numerous teams. The game continues until only one rider survives.

(b) May be played in the water, with riders mounting shoulders of horses.

(c) May be played by sides.

King of the Castle—One player chosen to be King assumes a position on a mound, tub, box, or stump. The King bids defiance to all foes by shouting:

> I'm King of the Castle;
> Get out, you cowardly rascal.

The other players assail the King, everyone being a claimant for the position of eminence. The King must protect the throne alone. Fair pulls and pushes are allowed, but players are not permitted to catch hold of the King's clothes. Penalty for such a foul is to be set aside as a prisoner of war—virtual expulsion from the game. The King may have an ally, who, however, does nothing except note fouls and expel those who commit them. The ally, therefore, is nothing more than a referee. The player who dethrones the King becomes King for next game.

Invisible Swat—Contestants are blindfolded and lie face down, heads toward each other. They grasp left hands. In their right hands they hold newspaper rolls or stockings stuffed with rags. They take turns swatting. "Are you there, Charlie?" shouts the one who is going to swat. The opponent must respond immediately with, "Here!" The swatter swats once! The swatee ducks, but must not let go the opponent's left hand. Count hits for a round of 5 or 10 swats.

TAG GAMES

Cross Tag—One player may save another from capture or take the play away from him by crossing between the player and It. Immediately, It pursues the runner who has crossed.

Clap In, Clap Out—Opposing teams line up at two ends of a playing space, being from 30' to 50' apart. One team sends a runner to the opposing side. The players on this side stand with both feet back of their line with one hand outstretched, palm up. The runner walks along this line. He taps each hand, in turn, until he decides which player he wants to chase him. He slaps this person's hand hard. Immediately he runs for his own line. If he gets there before the chaser can tag him he is safe. If not, he joins the other side. A runner may pretend to hit a hand hard but then hit it gently in order to throw his opponents off guard.

Maze Tag (Colonnade; Streets and Alleys)—Form 8 to 16 lines. Each line spaces off so that all Number Ones, Twos, and so forth, are in a straight line. Each person's hands should be able to touch the hands of the player on either side as they stand with arms straight out from the shoulder. Now space off similarly with the players in front and behind.

Players stand facing front with arms stretched out. This makes a series of aisles or streets. At the signal, all players, keeping their arms outstretched, make a quarter turn to the right. That makes new aisles. There is a runner and a chaser. Neither may break through any aisle or duck under. At each signal, there is the quarter turn to the right. A leader who uses the whistle wisely will make this a very interesting game.

When a player is tagged, another two are chosen to run.

Squirrel in a Tree—Players form groups of three. Two of each group join hands to form a "tree." The third gets between the two so that their arms enclose him. Two other players are the Dog and the Squirrel, respectively. The Dog chases the Squirrel, which may save itself by ducking into a tree. The player in that tree must immediately leave, with the Dog in pursuit. The fun comes in frequent changes. When the Dog catches a Squirrel, they exchange places.

Variations: (a) There may be several Squirrels without a home. At the signal, every Squirrel must get out of its tree and into another. The homeless Squirrels endeavor each time to find a home. This is a very lively game and a good mixer. After playing for awhile, the Squirrels may change places with players forming the trees, thus giving every player a chance to run.

(b) Three players may form the tree.

(c) **Bird in a Nest (Bird's Nest)**—The Birds run with arms spread out, as if they were flying.

Tunnel Race—Players form two concentric circles. Players in the two circles face each other and hold hands to form a tunnel. "It" walks around the circle and taps the clasped hands of two players. These two players immediately leave their position, and run in opposite directions inside the tunnel, trying to get back to their position. The tagger steps into one of the positions as soon as the runners leave. The player left out becomes It.

Japanese Tag—The player is required to hold one hand on the spot touched when tagged, until he or she tags another player. It is just too bad if the tag was on the heel.

Snatch—Players line up on 2 equal sides, facing one another, with about thirty feet between the 2 lines. Both lines of players number off from right to left. In the center of the space between the lines is placed a bottle or stick with a rag or handkerchief on it. Or it may be a stool, a wastebasket upside down, or a stump, with a beanbag or towel on it.

The leader calls a number. Both players bearing that number from the two sides rush out to the center. If one of the players is slow, the other snatches the rag and rushes back. If the opposing player can tag the player who has the rag before the runner can get back to his or her own lines, 1 point is scored for the tagging side. However, if the runner gets to the line with the rag without being tagged that side scores two points.

If both runners reach the center about the same time, they stall around, making fake grabs at the rag. Finally, when one player thinks the opponent is off guard, the player snatches the rag and runs for his or her own line.

Players soon learn that it is not a good idea to rush out and grab the rag immediately, since once the rag is touched, a player is liable to be tagged. It does not matter that the grab was unsuccessful. The other player may tag, or may snatch up the rag and rush for his or her own line.

Duck on a Rock—Each player finds a stone. Players may use beanbags instead of stones. One player is It, and places his or her stone (the duck) on a large rock (or stump) and stands by as guard. The other players stand at a line 15' to 20' away and toss their stones at the duck on the rock. When the duck is knocked off, the guard immediately replaces it. Players must take their position at the spots where their stones landed. When a player thinks there is a good chance to get back to the throwing line without being tagged, he or she snatches up the stone and dashes for safety. If the player is tagged by the guard, they exchange places. Players may only pretend to pick up their stones, but if they touch them, they become liable to be tagged.

The guard may not tag a runner when his or her own stone is off. So when the stone is knocked off, all players shout, "Duck off!" and dash for home. The guard must replace the duck before he or she can tag a runner who has picked up a stone.

If a player tosses a stone and it touches the stone of another player both players are allowed to return with their stones without danger of being tagged.

This is a great game for developing accuracy, daring, and alertness.

Still Pond—One player is blindfolded. The others scatter about the playground. The blindfolded player is placed at the center and the leader asks: "How many horses has your father in his stable?" "Three," the player replies. "What color are they?" "Black, white, and gray." "Turn around three times and catch whom you may." The blindfolded player is spun around three times and then says, "Still pond. No more moving." The other players must now stand still, being allowed to take three steps only. The blindfolded player begins to grope around and if he or she catches someone, must guess by touching the hair, dress, arm, etc., who is caught. If the player guesses correctly, the player caught becomes It. If the guess is incorrect, the search must continue. Players may stoop, dodge, or use any reasonable means to escape being caught, provided they do not move more than three steps.

Space Port (Prisoner's Base)—Players are evenly divided into two teams. Zones or bases are marked off by drawing lines 30' to 60' apart. In back of the lines, boxes 5' x 10' are drawn. These are the space ports.

The game begins when one side sends out a player to dare the opponents. One of the enemy starts in pursuit, and the player runs for his or her home space port. If the player is touched before reaching home, the player is captured and must immediately go to the opposing side's space port. A player may only tag an opponent who left home space port first, and can only be tagged by one who left afterward. When a player has captured an opponent, that player may return home untouched and is subject to capture only after making a fresh sally.

A prisoner may be released if a teammate runs the gauntlet of the enemy and touches the prisoner behind the enemy's line before being tagged. Such a release requires great skill, alertness, and deception. After the runner touches a prisoner the two are permitted to return unharmed to their home space port.

A prisoner is required to keep only one foot in the opponents' space port, and therefore may stretch toward a teammate to facilitate deliverance. When there are several prisoners, only one must have a foot touching the space port. Thus they may form a chain stretching toward

Space Port (Prisoner's Base)

the rescuer, but only one prisoner may be released at a time.

The game continues until all the players on one side are captured.

Pick-a-Stick (Similar to **Space Port**)—See diagram on page 127. The player to leave home last may tag any player of the opposing side who left home first.

If a player can get to the opponent's goal where the sticks are placed, the player picks one of them up and is free to take it back to his or her own goal, unmolested.

A tagged player becomes a prisoner. Prisoners may be rescued the same way sticks are taken. When some of a side's players have been captured, the team cannot take any sticks until it frees its prisoners. The first side to get all the sticks of the opposing side wins.

Four to six sticks are used in each goal. The field is 30' to 60' across from one goal to the other.

Fox and Geese (**Wheel Tag**)—This game is especially good in the snow. Clear off paths on a level surface like the spokes of a wheel (see illustration). Or mark off the wheel on the ground with lime, using a liner. The game also can be played indoors by using chairs and string to mark the spokes of the wheel. There may be more than one circle, one outside the other.

The player who is the fox chases the others, trying to tag someone. If the fox succeeds, they exchange places. Any player who runs out of the paths becomes the fox. The geese may jump across from one path to another, but the fox cannot. Neither can the fox tag a goose across the paths. Any goose who occupies the center is safe. However, only one goose can occupy the center at a time. The last one there takes possession and all the others must leave or be tagged.

Fox and Geese (Wheel Tag)

Mystery Tag—Players stand in a circle. Each player, hands extended with palms together, faces center. "It" walks around the circle, pretending to place a pebble in the hands of each player, and each player pretends to have received the pebble. The player who has really received it then breaks away from the circle, with the other players in pursuit. The player who succeeds in catching the one who holds the pebble then becomes It.

Squirrel Tails—Players are evenly divided into two or more teams. Each player has a strip of cloth (a tie or handkerchief) slipped under the back of the belt. At a signal, all players rush to a central point where there is a treasure—peanuts or candy of some kind. Players try to get some of this treasure and return with it to their home base. A player may be de-tailed by an opponent. This puts the player out of the game and makes void any treasure captured on that particular raid. Players are safe when home. Thus Squirrels will be alert to protect their tails while trying to capture the tails of opponents and at the same time pick up some of the treasure. At the end of the game each peanut or piece of candy counts 1 point. Each tail counts 5 points.

Drop the Hat—Two teams face each other. A hat is tossed in the air. If it comes down right side up, one team must run to its goal with the other team in pursuit. If it lands bottom side up, the other team runs to its goal line. Players tagged go to the opposing side.

Lame Wolf—One player is chosen to be the wolf. All the others are the "children." An area is marked off for the wolf's den. At the other end of the playing space an area is marked off for the children's house. The wolf goes to the den. The children run out of their house and begin to taunt the wolf, singing "Who's Afraid of the Big Bad Wolf?" or making jeering remarks: "Lame wolf can't catch anybody." When there is a good chance to catch someone, the wolf dashes out of the den in pursuit. However, the wolf can run only three steps when he or she must start hopping on one foot. Anyone caught becomes a lame wolf and must help catch the other children. When the rest of the children are safe at home the wolf and mates retire to their den. Again the children venture forth to taunt the wolf. The game continues until only one "child" remains. That player becomes the lame wolf for the next game. The wolf and the children may return at any time to their den or home to rest.

Dragon Tag—From 5 to 10 players link arms and become the dragon. They endeavor to encircle the other players, one or more at a time. When they do, the players thus caught add themselves to the dragon. This continues until all players are caught. Boundaries should be decided before the game begins.

Variation: (a) The last player in line places a handkerchief or towel in the back of his belt. The dragon begins to chase itself as the first player in line (the dragon's head) attempts to catch its tail.

(b) Several dragons can try to snatch one another's tails while trying to protect their own.

Dumbbell Tag—Players stand in a circle. "It" stands in the center. A dumbbell, ball, or other object is passed from one player to another. If It tags the player who has the dumbbell, that person becomes It.

Players must always receive the dumbbell when it is offered. They may move about freely. Players may pretend to pass the dumbbell one direction and pass it another.

Last Couple Out—Players line up as partners. The player who is It stands 8′ to 10′ ahead of the first set of partners, with his back to them. When It shouts, "Last couple out!" the last set of partners must move forward, one on either side of the line, with the idea of passing It and clasping hands in front of that player. They may come swiftly or slowly, and It may not turn to see them coming, but looks straight ahead. Only when they are even with It can he or she move. But when they are even, It dashes after them, trying to tag one of them before they can clasp hands. If It succeeds in tagging one of them, that player takes It's place, and the player who was It and the other partner become the lead couple. If the partners succeed in clasping hands, they become the new lead couple, and It tries again.

Pom Pom Pullaway—This is an old favorite. Two parallel lines, 30' to 50' apart, are drawn. Trees, sticks, or stones may be used to indicate the lines. Sometimes the curb of a city street serves the purpose. All players stand on or behind one of the lines, except It, who stands in the center of the playing field and shouts:

> Pom Pom Pullaway!
> If you don't come I'll pull you away.

At this, all players must leave the safety zone and run across to the opposite line. "It" tries to tag as many as possible before they reach the safety line. Anyone tagged joins It in catching other players as they dash across the open space. The game continues until all players are caught. The first player caught becomes It for the next game.

Variation: **Hill Dill**—Two lines are drawn across the playing space, 15' to 30' apart. "It" stands between the lines and calls: "GO!" The other players then run across the playing area to the other line. While running across this area, they may be tagged. When tagged, they help tag

others. The game continues until all players have been
caught.

Water Sprite—Two lines of players are located opposite
each other, 30′ to 60′ apart. The intervening space
represents the river. Between the two lines is It, the Water
Sprite, who beckons to one of the players to leave the
"bank." Immediately the Water Sprite must shut his or her
eyes and count to 10. The player signaled, in turn, signals
to a player on the opposite "bank" while the Sprite has the
eyes covered. These two players try to exchange positions
while the Water Sprite tries to tag one of them. If
successful, the player tagged becomes It.

Animal Chase—Two corners or areas are marked off as
pens. Players are named by groups—bears, dogs, cats,
sheep, wolves, rabbits, etc. "It," called the Chaser, stands
outside one of the pens. All other players stand inside the
pen. The Chaser calls the name of animals of any group,
and all the players bearing that name must rush for the
opposite pen. Any players caught must assist the Chaser in
tagging.

Bear and Guard—The "bear" sits on a chair or stool in
the center of a circle of players. A "guard" stands by the
bear. Players in the circle try to touch the bear without
being touched by the guard. The guard must keep one hand
on the chair, but can move all around it. Any player tagged
by the guard must take the bear's place.

Bell Ringer—Limits are decided. All the players but one
are blindfolded and scattered about the playing area. The
player who is not blindfolded carries a bell which must be
rung continuously. The blindfolded players try to catch the
player carrying the bell. The one who catches that player
becomes the bellringer. Players who are blindfolded

should be cautioned to hold their hands out in front of them to avoid painful collisions.

Sardines—One player hides in a closet, behind a door, under the steps, behind a big rock, or in a clump of trees or bushes, depending on the location. The rest scatter and hunt, each player hunting alone. Each player who finds the hidden player hides with him or her, being careful not to tip off the hiding place. If there are others near at the time, that player may go on as if still seeking and come back later at a favorable opportunity. Imagine the fun when ten or more players crowd into the same hiding place. The hunt continues until all the players find the hiding place. The last person to find the group becomes It.

I Spy—One player, It, leans the head, eyes shut, against home base, a tree, post, or wall, and counts to 100 thus: 5, 10, 15, 20, etc. The others scatter and hide. At 100, It shouts, "Here I come! Ready or not! All around base are It," and then tries to find the hiders. On finding one, It shouts, "I spy Johnny" (or whoever it is) and dashes for home. If the hider reaches home before It does, the hider is safe. Hiders also may sneak home while It's back is turned; they shout "Free" when they reach base. The first player caught is It the next time.

Variations: (a) **Throw the Club**—A club or stick is leaned against a post or wall. One player throws the club. While It is retrieving it and placing it back in position, all the players hide. "It" then goes out seeking the hiders. When It locates one of them he yells, "I spy Charley," and dashes for the club. If It reaches the club first the hider becomes a prisoner. If the hider beats It to the club, the hider throws it, and It must retrieve the stick and replace it before hunting the other players. When a player beats It to the club, that player may select one prisoner to be free to hide again. "It" must find all the hiders and make them prisoners.

(b) **Kick the Can**—This is the same game as **Throw the Club**, except that players kick a can instead of throwing a stick.

CIRCLE GAMES

Cat and Rat—This old game is a never-failing favorite. The players stand in a circle, holding hands. One player inside the circle is the rat. Another player outside the circle is the cat. The cat tries to catch the rat. The players help the rat and hinder the cat by raising or lowering their arms, not allowing the cat to break through the circle.

Variation: There may be more than one cat and one rat at a time.

Bull in the Ring—Players form a ring around the "bull," holding hands. The bull tries to break through, rushing, lunging, or pulling to break the ring. If the bull escapes, it is chased, and the player who catches it becomes bull in turn. It is not fair for the bull to duck under.

Variation: **Bear in the Net**—The object of the game is the same, except that the bear is allowed to duck under or plunge over the extended arms of the players.

Pin Guard—The players form a circle. One player at center attempts to guard a tenpin or soft-drink bottle. The other players toss a volleyball, basketball, or soccer ball at the pin, trying to knock it down. When a player is successful, that player takes the center player's place.

Variation: **Can Guard**—Instead of the pin, tin cans are set up at center, one on top of the other. When they are knocked down the center player must immediately replace them. The others shoot at that player with the ball until the cans are replaced and the player yells "Cans Up!"

During this procedure the players must not shoot at the cans but at the player. The player who knocked down the cans takes the center player's place for the next round.

Stormy Sea—Players find partners. Each set of partners selects the name of some fish, which they keep to themselves. There are two less chairs than players. One couple, the "Whales," walk about the room calling the names of fish. As they call Perch, Bass, Cat, Buffalo, Porpoise, Shark, Mackerel, Halibut, and other names, the partners with those names get up and follow the Whales. When the Whales shout, "Stormy sea!" everyone rushes for seats. One set of partners is left out and they become the Whales.

Variation: The game may be played outdoors by assigning partners to various trees, or by drawing small circles on the ground.

Slide Kelly Slide—Players sit in chairs placed close together in a circle. "It" stands inside the circle. When It calls, "Slide Kelly Slide," all players slide in the direction It points. As the players slide, It attempts to sit in a vacant chair. If successful, the player left standing becomes It.

Variation: **Ocean Wave**—There is one vacant chair. As It yells, "Slide left," or "Slide right," the players move to fill the vacant chair as it appears next to them. "It" dashes for the vacant seat and keeps after it until successful. The location of the vacant seat is constantly changing, for the players move into it as it comes next to them. If It gets a seat and the call has been "Slide left," the player to It's right becomes It.

Garden Scamp—All but two of the players form a circle. The space inside the circle is the garden. The Scamp is inside the circle; the Gardener is outside. The Gardener calls, "Who let you into my garden?" The Scamp replies, "I let myself into your garden." The Gardener then chases the Scamp, who dodges in and out of the cicle.

The Gardener must follow everywhere the Scamp goes, going through the same openings and doing the same things. When caught, the Scamp becomes the Gardener and has the privilege of choosing the next Scamp. The Scamp may do anything to make it more difficult for the Gardener—jump over clasped hands, play leapfrog with one of the players, or go through on hands and knees.

Kitty Wants a Corner—All players except one occupy chairs in a circle. The player who is It goes first to one player and then to another, saying "Kitty wants a corner." "Go to the next door neighbor," is the response. Any two players may signal each other and make an exchange of "corners." In fact, the players take a great delight in tantalizing Kitty by making frequent changes while It's attention is directed elsewhere. Kitty may feign lack of awareness of what is going on and then suddenly dash in to take a vacated corner. If successful, the player who is left out becomes It.

If it is too difficult to get a corner, Kitty may call, "Everybody change," whereupon each player must find a new corner. In the scramble, surely Kitty will succeed in getting a place.

Find Your Knee—This game is very active and not recommended for small children. Form 2 circles, one inside the other. Each player in the inner circle must have a partner in the outer circle. On the signal, the outer circle walks clockwise, while the inner circle walks counter-clockwise. At a signal to stop, players in the inner circle drop to one knee. Those in the outer circle must find their partners and sit on their knees. The last player to sit on his or her partner's knee is out.

Leaning Towers—Players join hands and make a circle. Number off 1-2, 1-2, etc. At a signal, all the 1s lean slowly toward the center of the circle; at the same time, all the 2s lean away from the center. A player's feet should be about shoulder-width apart. Players are to lean in or out without bending at the waist. After a few practices, try switching more rapidly.

Have You Seen My Sheep?—Players form a circle. One player is Shepherd. The Shepherd walks around outside the circle, taps a player on the back and asks, "Have you seen my sheep?" That player asks, "What does it look like?" The Shepherd then describes someone in the circle: "He wears a blue tie, a brown coat, and brown shoes"; or, "A blonde with a good disposition, blue eyes, a square chin." The player tries to guess who is being described. If the guess is correct, the Shepherd says, "Right," and the guesser chases the one described. Both must run outside the circle. If the chaser catches the runner before the runner can get back to his or her position, the chaser becomes the Shepherd. If not, the runner becomes Shepherd. The Shepherd does not run.

Untie the Knot—Groups of ten (always an even number) players stand in a circle, shoulder to shoulder. Each player is to reach with the right hand and grasp the hand of the player directly across the circle. Then each player reaches and grasps the left hand of any other player in the circle. At a signal, the group is to untie the knot. They cannot let go at any time, but can pivot by using the palms of the hands. The first group to untie the knot successfully wins.

Postman—Players sit in chairs in a circle. Each is given the name of a city. One player stands in the center as postman. The leader is postmaster. The postmaster calls the names of 2 cities: New York to Dallas, for instance.

Players named New York and Dallas must immediately arise and exchange seats. The postman tries to catch one of them or attempts to sit in a vacated chair. The player who is caught becomes postman. Players are not allowed to step outside the circle of chairs. If the postman seems to have great difficulty capturing someone, the leader may call as many as 4 or 5 cities at a time, thus making it almost certain that someone will be caught. The announcement, Parcel Post! means that all players must change seats.

How Do You Like Your Neighbors?—Players sit in chairs in a circle. It, standing in the center, points to someone and says, "How do you like your neighbors?" "Oh, not so well," comes the response. "Who would you like better?" The player must name two other people in the room. Those two must change places immediately with the undesired neighbors while It tries to take one of the empty seats. The player left out is It and the game proceeds. If the player to whom the question is put answers "Fine," or some reply indicating satisfaction, there must be a general scramble in which *all* players change seats. In this mix-up, It usually finds a seat.

Keyed Up—Players are seated in a circle. There are just enough chairs to seat everyone, except one player, who stands inside the circle. That person has a bunch of keys on a key ring. He or she starts walking around the inside of the circle, and then signals to one player who is seated. That player gets up and follows. The second player beckons to another player, who falls into line behind the other two. So it goes until a number are walking around inside the circle. Suddenly the leader drops the bunch of keys. That is the signal for every player to try to take a seat. The player left out becomes the leader for the next round.

Number Call—Players are numbered. "It" is blind-folded. "It" calls from 2 to 4 numbers and those players must change seats. "It" tries to either tag a player or occupy a vacated seat. Players whose numbers are called proceed immediately to exchange seats, dodging or moving stealthily as may be required to keep from being tagged. If caught, the player must become It and the game proceeds, It taking the number of the caught player.

Variations: (a) **Fruit Basket Turnover**—Each player is named for a fruit (peach, banana, orange, apple, etc.). "It" calls out the names of two fruits. Those players attempt to exchange seats, and It tries to occupy the empty seat. When It calls out, "Fruit basket turnover!" everyone changes places and It tries to get an empty seat. The player left standing is It.

(b) **General Delivery**—Each player is given the name of a city. "It" calls out two cities, and while the players with those names try to change seats, It attempts to get to an empty seat. "It" may call, "General Delivery!" and everyone must change seats.

Going to Jerusalem—This is an old favorite. Chairs are set in a single row, facing alternately first one way and then the other. There are fewer chairs than players. Someone plays the piano as all players march around the chairs, keeping time to the music and hands off the chairs. Suddenly the music stops and players scramble to sit in the chairs. Players are not allowed to turn a chair around. Those left without a chair drop out and the game proceeds. Each time the music stops, another chair is taken away. Finally two players march around the 1 remaining chair. Much depends on the pianist, who should stop at unexpected intervals.

Variations: (a) Arrange the chairs in two rows back to back.

(b) Arrange the chairs in a circle facing in. Sometimes called **Musical Chairs**.

(c) Arrange the chairs in a circle facing out.

Bus Ride—Players are seated in two rows of chairs, facing one another, with 6 to 8 feet separating the rows. The rows represent the seats on an old-fashioned side-seated bus.

One player is conductor and calls various stops. If a numbered street is called, all players must get up and exchange sides. If a name with "street" attached is called, the players do not move. If a Road is called all players must get up and run around their row of chairs and try to get a chair, any chair. The conductor also tries to get a chair. The person left out becomes the conductor.

Stagecoach—Players are seated in a circle. Each one is given the name of some part of the stagecoach—wheel, hub, axle, seat, door, harness, brake, horses, driver, passengers, baggage, spoke, tire, step. One player begins telling a story about a stagecoach, mentioning all the different things related to the coach. As each thing is mentioned, the player (or players) representing it gets up and runs around his or her own chair. At some point in the story, the storyteller shouts "Stagecoach!" and everyone must change seats. The storyteller tries to get a seat in the scramble, thus leaving another player to begin a new story.

Variation: **Auto Trip**—Players are named for automobile parts. The storyteller tells a story of an auto trip. "We got out the old bus and had the 'tank' filled with 'gas.' Air was pumped into the 'tires.' A 'spare' was in the trunk. I pressed the 'starter' and we were off. The 'door' rattled, the 'engine' shook, the 'hood' came loose, etc." The parts mentioned get up and follow the storyteller, who suddenly yells, "Blowout," and each player must scramble for a seat. The player left out becomes the next storyteller.

Drop the Handkerchief—This old-timer is always fun. Players form a circle. One player walks around outside the circle with a handkerchief or rag. Player One drops it behind player Two and keeps on moving around the circle, endeavoring to walk all the way around before player Two discovers it. If successful, player Two must stand in the center of the circle. But if player Two discovers the handkerchief, he or she starts in pursuit of player One. If Two catches One, One goes to the center. The new runner now walks around the circle. A player in the center may be rescued if another player tosses the handkerchief inside the circle. The player in the center then immediately starts in pursuit.

Variation: Play the game to music. When the music is slow, the runners move slowly. When the music is fast, the runners speed up. When it stops, they stop. Penalty for failing to obey instructions means going to the center.

Flying Dutchman—Players find partners and form a circle. Partners hold hands. One couple outside the circle hold hands as they start to run around the circle. They slap the hands of some couple in the circle and continue around. The partners touched immediately start running in the opposite direction, holding hands as they run. When the couples meet it may take some maneuvering to avoid a collision. The first pair back to the vacated position remains in the circle. The pair left out continues the game.

Variations: (a) Running couples stop when they meet. They shake hands, bow, and say, "Howdy." Immediately thereafter they dash madly around the rest of the circle.

(b) Partners perform some stunt when they meet. For instance, they may be required to hold hands and swing around once. Or each person may be required to place the forefinger on the head and whirl around three times.

In the Pond—A good game for a picnic. Players stand in a straight line or circle with the leader giving directions. When the leader calls, "In the pond," all players must jump forward one jump. If the leader calls, "On the bank," while the group is "in the pond" they all jump backward one jump. If the group is "in the pond" and the leader calls, "In the pond," players must remain stationary. The leader may confuse the group by jumping contrary to the command. Players making mistakes drop out.

Simon Says—Players stand about with plenty of room between each player for action. The leader calls commands, such as, "Simon says, 'Hands on hips and body bend.' " "Simon says, 'Hands raise.' " "Simon says, 'Position, and jump forward.' " Players obey commands of the leader. However, if the command is not preceded with "Simon says," the players do nothing. Any player failing to obey a "Simon says" command immediately, or any obeying a command not prefaced by "Simon says" must drop out. The leader makes it more confusing by going through the action each time.

Variations: (a) **I Say Stand**—The leader shouts, "I say stand," at which command all players must stand. "I say stoop," and all players must stoop. The orders are given in rapid succession. But the leader does not always fit the action to the command, saying, "I say stand," and at the same time assuming the stooping position. Any player who makes a mistake is out. No order should be obeyed unless the leader prefaces it by "I say."

(b) **Do This, Do That**—When the leader commands, "Do this," all players must imitate the action. But if the leader says, "Do that," players who imitate the action are dropped out of the game. The leader may play a violin, a piano, a flute, or other musical instrument, dance, skate, saw, sweep, fly, hammer, bat, kick a football.

Wink—This is an old-timer. In Harbin's boyhood days, this was a favorite. Chairs are arranged around the room with a boy behind each chair. Girls sit in all but one of the chairs. Each boy keeps his hands on the back of his chair, except when trying to prevent the girl sitting there from leaving. The boy with the empty chair makes an effort to get a partner by winking at the girls. When he winks at a girl she must immediately try to get up and move to his chair. The boy in whose chair she is sitting tries to prevent her from getting up. If he puts his hands on her shoulders before she rises, she must stay. The winker keeps at it until he succeeds in getting someone's partner.

Swat the Fly—Players form a circle with one player inside. A wastebasket or other suitable receptacle is in the center of the circle. The center player holds a roll of paper and walks around the circle. This player finally swats someone and immediately runs to deposit the roll of paper in the wastebasket. The person swatted pursues, picks up the roll, and tries to swat the runner before he or she can get back to the vacated place in the circle. The game continues with a new swatter.

Three Deep—Players form 2 circles, one inside the other, facing center. They do not hold hands. Two players on the outside of the circle and at some distance from each other begin the game as runner and chaser. The runner may keep from being tagged by stepping in front of one of the pairs of players, thus making the circle at that point 3 deep. The outside player of the three must immediately leave or be tagged. A player who is tagged becomes the chaser. A runner may run in any direction to the right or left or across the circle. However, the runner can only step in front of a player and make the circle three deep by moving inside the circle and to the right.

Variations: (a) **Two Deep**—Single circle. The runner may step in front of another player, whereupon that player must run.

(b) **Four Deep**—When the crowd is large, players may stand in rows of three.

(c) **Hook On**—Players stand about the playing space in partners, arms linked. The outside arms are held with elbows out. The runner may link onto one of the partners, whereupon the other must leave immediately to keep from being caught.

Jacob and Rachel—Form a circle, with two players inside. One player is blindfolded and takes the part of Jacob. Another player is Rachel. Jacob calls, "Rachel, where are you?" Rachel must immediately answer, "Here I am, Jacob," then dart to some other part of the circle to avoid being captured. Jacob may call as often as desired. Rachel must answer each time.

Variations: (a) Two Jacobs and two Rachels. Jacobs keep their hands extended all the time to avoid head-on collisions.

(b) Blindfold Rachel as well as Jacob. The hands-out rule would be advisable again.

Spin the Platter—Players form a circle. Each player is numbered. "It," in the center, calls a number as he or she starts to spin a tin plate. The player whose number is called must catch the plate before it stops spinning. Failure to do so makes that player It. If the plate is caught, the spinner must try again until someone misses.

Variation: (a) Player drops a cane by taking finger off top of cane, calling a number. Cane must be caught before it falls.

(b) Player bounces a ball which must be caught before it bounces a second time.

6

FUN WITH NONSENSE GAMES

The games in this section are just for fun. The participants sometimes end up in ridiculous positions and poses. Many do not enjoy these frivolous activities, but some do. Use your discretion in involving people in these games. Be sure all are good sports.

PRANKS AND PUZZLES

Inchy-pinchy—Everyone sits in a circle (not more than 15 to a group). The leader tells everyone to just go along with the game, and if they discover what is happening, not to reveal it to anyone else. Secretly, the leader has placed lipstick or colored chalk on his or her thumb and index finger. When the game begins, the leader turns to the left, gently pinches the neighboring player's cheek, and says, "Inchy-pinchy." This leaves a mark on the player's cheek. The player turns and repeats the act to the next player, and so on around until the leader's cheek is pinched. The leader continues to pinch the first player on the cheeks, forehead, nose, and chin, leaving marks all over his or her face.

My Grandmother Doesn't Like Tea—The leader announces, "My grandmother doesn't like tea, but she likes coffee." It goes from player to player, each saying, "My grandmother doesn't like tea, but she likes——." If a player calls any word with the letter T in it, the leader says, "No, she doesn't like that. She likes pears, but she doesn't like grapefruit." She doesn't like tea; therefore she doesn't like anything with the letter T in it. It will begin to dawn on some of the players as the game proceeds.

Crossed and Uncrossed—Players are seated in a circle. They are to pass around a pair of scissors. The first player passes them on, saying, "I receive them crossed and pass them uncrossed." The words "crossed" and "uncrossed" refer to the passers' legs or feet, though the uninitiated invariably think they refer to the scissors. If the feet are crossed when the scissors are received, and also when they are passed on, the player says, "I receive them crossed and pass them crossed."

He Can Do Little Who Cannot Do This—The leader holds a stick in the left hand. Thumping the floor with the stick, the leader says, "He can do little who cannot do this." Then the stick is handed to the next player who tries to do exactly as the leader has done. The chances are the player will fail. The trick lies in the fact that the leader holds the stick in the left hand. It is passed to the right, so the next player will probably hold it in the right hand. The game continues until the secret is discovered.

Magic Animal Cage—Invite guests to view the magic animal cage, in which will appear any animal the person can name. Prepare an elaborate build-up. A large mirror has been covered with a sheet to disguise its real identity and to make it look like a cage. Guests are brought in one at a time and asked what animal they would like to see. Whatever the answer, remove the drapery and let the guest look in the mirror.

It—One or more persons not familiar with the game are invited to go out of the room. The rest decide that It is always the person to the right. One at a time, the persons who were sent out of the room come back and try by questioning to discover who or what It is. One question only may be asked of a player, and they must be questions that can be answered by Yes or No. The answers will be very confusing, and the crowd will be greatly amused by the bewildered expression on the faces of the questioners. Example: "Is It human?" "Yes, I think so." "Is It a man?" "No." "Is It a woman?" "No."

MERRY MIX-UPS

Initial Information—Slips of paper are prepared, one for each player. At the top of the paper have been written the initials of different people who will be present. Under this is a series of questions which the player drawing the paper is to answer. The papers are shuffled and handed out, or players may be allowed to make a blind draw.

The answers must consist of only as many words as there are initials at the top of the sheet, and the words must begin with the initials in their proper order. Example:

E.S.D.

To whom does this paper belong? Ernest S. Doe

What is his character? Easy-going, sweet, desperate

What is his present occupation? Entertaining sweet dumbbelles

What are his suppressed desires? Evangelist, sculptor, Don Juan

What kind of hair has he? Extinct soft down

What kind of books does he prefer? Enlivening slippery detective

What animals are his favorites? Erratic slim dachshunds

What does he think of the opposite sex? Exquisite sweet darlings

What does he think of the world in general? Execrable, sordid, dumb

What do you predict for his future? Earning swell dividends

Consequences—Each player is given a piece of paper and a pencil. First, each writes an adjective or two describing a woman. The top of the paper is then folded down to prevent anyone seeing what has been written. It is passed to the right and the next person writes a woman's name. This goes on until the story is finished. The papers are then opened and read aloud to the group. The following information may be requested by the leader, or it may be typed on the sheets of paper before they are given to the players:

> An adjective describing a woman
> A woman's name
> An adjective describing a man
> A man's name
> Where they met
> What she did
> What he did
> What she said
> What he said
> The results
> What the world said

Description—Give the guests pencils and sheets of paper with a guest's name written on each sheet, together with 3 or 4 questions. Each guest is to describe the person by using the first initial of each of the person's names (first, middle, and last). Example:

> Carol Leigh Robert
> What is she like? *C*razy, *L*ovable, *R*omantic
> How does she walk? *C*rooked, *L*azy, *R*acey
> What does she eat? *C*orn, *L*ettuce, *R*elish

Confessions—One person whispers the name of a different person to each guest. Another person whispers to each guest a different location—in a tree, on the roof, in the swimming pool, on the beach, in a taxi, on the Queen Mary, in church, in Cincinnati. Still a third person whispers a different activity to each guest—singing swinging songs, eating peanuts, dancing the Highland fling, listening to the katydids, suffering heroically. The guests must "confess" who they were with, where they were, and what they were doing.

The results will naturally bring some ridiculous combinations. Imagine the uproar when one of the most sedate ladies in the group announces that she was sitting on top of the house, eating peanuts with the preacher.

Results—One leader whispers to each person the name of a different object. Another whispers something they are to do with the object. A third person whispers the consequences of such action. The fun of it arises from the fact that none of the three knows what the others have said. Some ridiculous combinations result, such as, "I was told to take a piano and hit Mr. Brown with it. All's well that ends well."

Problems and Answers—Did you ever hear anyone say, "What would you do if———?" All right! What would you? Give half the crowd slips of paper saying, "What would you do if ———?" They are to fill in the rest of the question.

To the other half of the crowd, give slips of paper saying, "I would ———." They are to write in a proposed line of action.

The slips are dropped into two containers, one for the problems and the other for the answers. Two people draw slips—one from the problems and the other from the answers. The problem is then read and the solution offered.

Variation: One group of players may be numbered for the problems, and another group for the answers. Number One reads a problem and Number One on the other side reads the proposed action.

Story Mix-up—Copy two short stories such as "Chicken Little" or "Red Riding Hood" on separate slips of paper, one sentence to a slip. Mix them up in a hat and then have each player draw a slip or two, according to the size of the crowd. Indicate one person to begin the story. The person to the right of the starter reads another sentence, and so on it goes around the circle. Naturally, there will be ridiculous combinations.

Cross Questions and Silly Answers—Players sit in two rows, facing one another. One person gives each player on one side a different question. Another person gives each player on the other side a different answer. Since neither knows what the other is saying you can imagine the results when the questions and answers begin to fall. The first player on one side asks the question assigned to him and the player opposite gives the answer that was whispered to her. "What is your hobby?" asks Number One. "No, no, a thousand times no!" comes the response from the player opposite. "Do you think the moon is made of green cheese?" asks Number Two. "We'll fight it out on this line if it takes all summer," comes the response.

Similarities—One person goes around the group whispering to each player the name of a different person present. Another whispers the name of different objects, animals, or insects. Each person is now required to tell why the person whose name was whispered is like the object suggested by the second whisperer. For instance, the first whisperer whispers to Mary the name Jack Brown. The second whisperer whispers "caterpillar." At the proper time, Mary must explain why "caterpillar" is an appropriate designation for Jack Brown. She may say, "Because he's a worm." Or she may feel in a complimentary mood and say, "Because he has possibilities of beauty."

Doctored Nursery Rhymes—In a mentally alert group, plenty of fun can be had by working out original endings for well-known nursery rhymes. Changes may be inserted after the first line:

> Mary had a little lamb,
> With green peas on the side;
> And when her escort saw the check,
> The poor boob nearly died.

> Jack Spratt could eat no fat,
> His wife could eat no lean;
> And so the question before the house
> Is "Who orders the meat, man or mouse?"

Sometimes the last line of the rhyme is changed with no effort at rhyming:

> Peter, Peter, pumpkin eater,
> Had a wife and couldn't keep her;
> He put her in a pumpkin shell—
> Well, how'd *you* like hobnobbing with a jack-o'-lantern?

Mystery Rhymes—This is fun for a small group. Even a large crowd could be divided into numerous small groups and enjoy it. Player One writes a line of poetry and folds it over so that no one can see what was written. Player Two is told the last word, so that the next line can be rhymed. One may also indicate the meter, saying:

> Da-da, da-da, da-da, da-da,
> Da-da, da-da, da-da, da-da.

Player Three writes another line in the same meter, if possible. The fourth line may rhyme with the third. For nonsense rhymes this ought to score tops.

Variation: **Mystery Advertising**—In this case each of the four players is given a word with which to end a line. The words may rhyme in couplets, if desired. Thus, the four words might be *fair, rare, style,* and *smile.* The rhyme must advertise some announced product, organization, or movement.

SILLY CIRCLES

Going to Texas—The leader announces that everyone in the group is going to Texas and that each person is allowed to take one article. One player starts by saying, "I will take my hat." Others decide to take an auto, a lamp, a suitcase, a toothbrush, a fan, a six-shooter, etc. When each person has named an article, player One is asked by the leader what will be done with the hat. One answers, "I will wear it," and pretends to put on a hat. Number Two must now repeat, "I will wear my auto"; Number Three, "I will wear my lamp," and so on, each player pretending to put on a hat. When this has been around, the leader asks Number Two about the auto. Two answers, "I will drive my auto," acting out driving. Again each player in turn must repeat, "I will drive my lamp," etc. This is repeated until all players have told what they will do with their articles and have repeated the action with the articles they have named.

Variation: Each person must repeat each item previously said and then tell his or her own item.

Do This and More—One player begins the game by doing something such as putting the thumbs to the ears and wiggling the fingers. One points to another player who must repeat that action and add another, such as putting the hand under the chin and wiggling the fingers. The next player may add sticking out the tongue. Each successive player must repeat, in order, all the actions of the other players and add another. No player may be called on more than once unless the player requests it.

Uncle Ned is Dead—This is a good game for a small group. If you want to use it with a large crowd, either divide into small groups or have a group of about 10 players play it while the rest observe the fun.

Players sit in a circle. One player begins by saying to the player to the right, "Uncle Ned is dead." That player asks, "How did he die?" "By closing his eye," is the reply, and the first player suits the action to the word by closing one eye. Then player Two turns to the player to the right and repeats the conversation. And so it goes around the circle until all players have one eye closed. Again One starts by saying, "Uncle Ned is dead." This time in answer to the question, "How did he die?" he answers, "By closing his eye, with his face awry." When that has gone around, player One begins again. The third time, the answer is "By closing his eye, with his face awry, and his foot up high"; the fourth time, "By closing his eye, with his face awry, his foot up high, and waving goodbye." Each time the additional grimace, posture, or motion is assumed and kept to the end. After the fourth round, the leader shouts, "He's buried!" and the game is ended.

Does She Cackle?—Players sit in a row or circle. Player One turns to the player to the right and says, "Want to buy a hen?" That player responds, "Does she cackle?" "She cackles," the first player replies. Number Two turns to Three and says, "Want to buy a hen?" Three asks, "Does she cackle?" Two then asks One, "Does she cackle?" One replies, "She cackles." Two turns to Three and repeats, "She cackles." Thus it goes all around the circle, Three speaking to Four, and so on. Each time the question "Does she cackle?" is relayed back to One, and the reply, "She cackles," is passed on to the last player consulted about buying a hen.

Variations: (a) Players must know names and use them: "Margy Jones said that Tom Clark said that Pearl Brown said that Bill Sims said that May Temple said, 'Want to buy a hen?' " The relay back would also carry all names.

(b) "Want to buy a duck?" "Does she quack?" "She quacks." "How does she quack?" "Quack-quack!" (player imitates a duck). Cats, dogs, and other animals may be used in the same manner.

(c) "Have you seen my flute?" "Does it toot?" "It toots." "How does it toot?" "Tweedle-weedle-weet." Other musical instruments may be used.

Wagging Fans—Players stand in a circle. The leader says to player One on the right, "My ship has come home from China!" Player One asks, "What has it brought?" "A fan," the leader replies, and pretends to fan with the right hand. Everyone in the circle imitates the leader's motion. Player One then says to the neighbor to the right, "My ship has come home from China." Again the question, "What has it brought? 'Two fans,' is the reply. Whereupon, Player One fans himself with both hands, and everyone follows the gesture. The statement, "My ship has come from China," and the question, "What has it brought?" continue from one player to another. Player Three, announcing that a ship has brought 3 fans, moves the right foot as well as the 2 hands, everyone else doing the same thing. At "4 fans" all move both hands and feet, stepping in place. At "5 fans," the hands, feet and right eyelid; at "6 fans" the hands, feet, and both eyelids; at "7 fans," the hands, feet, eyelids, and mouth; at "8 fans," the hands, feet, eyelids, mouth and head. By this time the whole company is a group of wagging fans. Persons who fail to keep up with the movements must pay forfeits.

Do You Know Joe Blow?—Players are seated in a circle. One player turns to the left-hand neighbor and asks, "Do you know Joe Blow?" That player answers, "No! How does he go?" The first player replies, "So," and starts patting the knee with the right hand.

The second player now turns to the person to the left and goes through the same process. So it continues until it gets back to the leader.

The leader starts all over again with the same series of questions, this time patting the left knee with the left hand. The next time around, he or she lifts the right knee and taps the floor with the right foot, then the left knee and the left foot. Next the leader jumps up and down. All players keep up all movements after once starting them. When the leader shouts, "Joe Blow's pooped!" everyone stops. If this doesn't loosen up your crowd, they are hopeless.

My Ship Came In—The players are seated about the room or campfire. The leader says to player Number One on the right, "My ship came in." "What did it bring?" asks One. "A fan," replies the leader, and begins a fanning motion. One turns to Number Two and the conversation is repeated. And so it goes all the way around the circle, all players keeping up the fanning. Now the leader repeats, "My ship came in." "What did it bring?" this time brings the response, "A pair of scissors," and the leader uses the middle and index fingers of the other hand to imitate a pair of scissors. Next comes a pair of shoes, and the feet are set in motion. Then a pair of glasses, with the eyes blinking; false teeth, with the mouth opening and closing, the teeth being displayed. Finally, a hat, with the head bobbing back and forth. That will probably leave the group limp, for all motions, once started, must be continued.

One Frog—Participants sit in a circle. It is more fun to have several circles, with about 10 players in each. The leader begins by saying, "One frog." The next player says, "One head." The third player says, "Two eyes." The fourth player says, "Four legs." The fifth player says, "In a pond." The sixth player says, "Kerplunk!" The seventh player begins again with, "Two frogs." The next player says, "Two heads." The sequence continues with Four eyes, Eight legs, In a pond, In a pond, Kerplunk! and Kerplunk! Notice that In a pond, and Kerplunk! are repeated by succeeding players as the game goes on. The game continues as long as no mistakes are made or until 5 frogs are completed. Should someone make a mistake by calling out the wrong words, that person must begin the game all over again with "One frog." Players cannot help one another with a sequence. Competition between teams can be fun.

Checkerberry On—Players stand in a circle facing each other. Each player is to think of a certain movement—saluting, waving a hand, patting a knee, rubbing an ear, or whatever. The motion must follow the rhythm of "Checkerberry, Checkerberry, Checkerberry, On." Everyone should practice the motion along with the chant to get the right rhythm. No two people standing together can have the same motion. Each player is to watch the neighbor on his or her right. The game begins with everyone chanting and clapping their hands to the rhythm. When they say the word "On," they all begin their movements. When they say the next "On," they all begin the motions their neighbors have just been performing. This continues around each time the word "On" is said. Anyone who breaks the sequence or does not perform the right motion must drop out. Each new start must begin again with the original movements.

Animal Rhythm—Each group should be limited to 8 to 10 players. The players sit in a circle. Each player is assigned a particular animal motion. Suggestions:

Monkey—lift arm in the air and scratch underneath arm with other hand.

Snake—place palms together and move arms in wiggling motion away from body.

Bird—flap hands like wings.

Deer—place extended fingers beside head, making antlers.

Giraffe—raise arm and point hand down to represent giraffe's neck and head.

Goat—make goatee by placing hand under chin and wiggling fingers.

Alligator—extend arms straight out, palms together, move hands up and down to represent jaws of alligator.

Elephant—make fists, place one on top of other, and raise to nose.

Fish—pucker lips, open and close to imitate fish.

Wolf—howl like a wolf.

In rhythm, pat knees twice, then snap fingers twice. While everyone else is doing this, the leader does his or her own animal movement as the knees are patted, then does another animal movement as the fingers are snapped. The person whose motion the leader has acted out then does his or her own motion as the knees are patted, then some other animal motion as the fingers are snapped. This process goes on until someone makes a mistake. That person then goes to the end of the line and the leader starts over. Everyone who moves up a seat must assume the motion assigned to that particular seat. The object is to get the leader out.

Zoo Antics—All players except the leader form a circle. Demonstrate to the group the various animal antics that will be required during the game. The object of the game is to get someone else to be It. The leader points to a player and calls out the name of an animal. The player pointed to and the players on either side must respond before the leader counts to ten. If they respond correctly, the leader goes to someone else; if not, the player who fails to do the right motion becomes It. Suggestions:

Elephant—player pointed to makes a trunk by placing joined fists on nose. The player's partners, the people to the left and right, place their open hands, palms out, beside the player's head to make elephant's ears.

Fish—player pointed to puckers lips like a fish. The players on either side place their palms together and make wiggling motions away from their bodies to represent a fish swimming.

Kangaroo—player pointed to makes a pouch by cupping hands together and holding them in front of the stomach. The players on either side jump up and down.

Goat—player pointed to makes a goatee by placing hand under the chin and wiggling fingers. The players on either side place their index fingers on player's head for horns.

Variation: **The Spirit of '76**—Although not a zoo animal, this presents a challenge: player pointed to pretends to hold a flag, while player on the right pretends to play a fife, and the one on the left, a drum.

A What?—Players sit in a circle, not more than 10 or 15 to a group. The leader takes an object (a key, pencil, pen, coin, etc.) and hands it to the player on the left and says, "This is a key!" The player, Number One, responds, "A what?" "A key!" replies the leader. "Oh, a key!" says

Number One, and takes the key. Number One then turns and says, "This is a key," to his or her neighbor on the left, Number Two, who in turn responds, "A what?" Number One turns to the leader and says, "A what?" The leader replies, "A key!" Number One turns back to Number Two and replies, "A key!" Number Two says, "Oh, a key!" takes the key, turns to Number Three, and says, "This is a key." This continues all the way around the circle. Meanwhile, the leader has started a different object around the circle to the right. The players respond in the same way: "A what?" and so on. The fun begins when the objects meet and pass each other.

Variation: Make up other names for the objects—a dog and a hog; a bat and a cat; a grizzly gorilla and a slimy salamander.

I Saw a Ghost—Players line up in a single line. The leader, standing at one end of the line, says, "I saw a ghost and he went like this," making this sound as mysterious as possible, and kneels. All players follow suit, doing whatever the leader does. Again the leader speaks, this time extending both hands straight out in front; next time, lifting the left leg in the air. The next time, the leader suddenly shoves the next player sharply. As a result, the whole crowd goes down like a pack of cards.

ANIMATED ANTICS

Statues—All players stand in a line, except one, who stands some distance ahead of the line, covers the eyes, and counts from 1 to 10. The players try to get from one side of the room to the other while It is counting. When It reaches 10 and looks up suddenly, any player caught in motion must go back to the starting point. The others hold whatever position they happen to have at the time, statuelike. The first player to cross the room becomes It, or has the privilege of selecting the next It.

Shadow Bluff—All players but It gather in a room over the door of which a sheet has been drawn. A light is so arranged that shadow pictures can be made on the sheet. It sits on the opposite side of the sheet in a dark room and tries to identify the players whose shadows appear on the screen. These players must appear one at a time. They are privileged to use simple disguise, such as false paper noses or ears, funny hats, paper curls, etc. They may make any gestures they desire. When the guesser identifies a shadow correctly, the person whose identity is guessed becomes It.

Variation: May be used as a team game. The number of correct guesses would be the score.

Poor Kitty—This old-timer wears well. Players are seated about the room. One player has a pillow. If a boy, he puts the pillow down in front of a girl, kneels on it, and meows three times, as plaintively as he can. The girl must hold a solemn countenance as she pats him on the head each of the three times and say consolingly, "Poor little kitty." If she laughs she takes the kitty's place. Girls must kneel before boys. Player continues until a patter laughs.

Pyramid Candle Bowling—Place 10 candles, set up like tenpins, on a board or piece of cardboard. Light the candles. Place a chin rest of two or three books in front of the candles. Each player tries to blow out the candles. Two blows are allowed. Scoring is done as in bowling. Blowing all the candles out at the first blow is a strike, and the blower scores 10 points, plus all the points in the next two tries in the second frame. Blowing all 10 candles out in the 2 blows in a frame is a spare and the player scores 10, plus all that he or she blows out on the first turn in the next frame. Players may compete singly or in teams.

Variation: Players may be given one blow to see who can blow out the most.

Apple Race—Contestants are required to balance an apple on top of the head and walk to a goal line. If the apple falls off, the player must go back to the starting point and begin again.

Spooning Race—Form partners. Each couple is furnished with 2 spoons tied together with a string 6″ long. One dish of ice cream is provided for each couple. Using the tied spoons, they eat the ice cream as quickly as possible.

File Chair Relay—Teams of 5 to 10 players sit in chairs arranged in a row. The first player rises and runs around the entire row, back to the original chair. As soon as player One sits down, player Two gets up and makes the circuit. So it goes until each player has been entirely around. First team to finish wins.

Variation: As soon as player One passes Two, that player gets up and follows. Three follows Two, and so on, until each player has made the circuit and is seated.

Dropping Peanuts—Contestants stand erect and drop, from chest height, 15 peanuts, one at a time, into a glass jar.

Dropping Clothespins—Contestants kneel on a chair. From the top of the back of the chair they try to drop clothespins into a narrow-mouthed jar.

Tossing Peanuts—Contestants try to toss peanuts into a jar or coffee can placed 6′ away.

Pillowcase Relay—Form teams of 10 players each. Each team is provided with a pillow. At the signal the first player on each team takes the pillow out of the case, then puts it back and hands it to the next player, who does the same. It goes down the line until each player has taken the pillow out of its case and put it back. First team finished wins.

Run and Pop—Form teams of 5 to 10 players each. As many paper bags as there are players are placed on chairs at the end of the room (one chair for each team). The first player on each team runs to their chair, blows up a bag, bursts it, and returns to touch the next player on the team. A runner must not leave the starting point until he or she has been touched by the preceding runner.

Stand and Pop—Teams of 10 players each stand single file, each player holding an unopened paper bag in the right hand. At the signal, the last player in line on each side blows up the sack and pops it on the back of the player immediately in front. As soon as the first bag is popped, player Two blows up a bag and pops it on the back of player Three. Player Ten pops the sack on his or her knee.

Right Foot, Left Foot—Teams of 10 players each stand single file with a paper bag under each foot. At the signal, the last player in line reaches down, picks up the sack under the right foot, blows it up, pops it, and immediately tags player Two, directly in front. Player Two goes through the same performance. As soon as player Ten pops the sack under the right foot, the one under the left foot is picked up and popped. This is the signal for player Nine to pop the sack under the left foot, and so on back down the line until player One has popped the left-foot sack.

Fireworks—Players are divided into two equal teams. At a given goal there is a sack for each player. On signal, there is a grand rush for the goal, where each player must blow up a sack and pop it. The first team finished wins.

Hammer Throw—A paper bag is blown up and tied with a string. The string should be from 36″ to 40″ long. Players must hold the end of the string and throw the sack as far as they can. Chances are, it will not be very far.

Apple Bite—Apples are tied on strings attached to a heavy cord that is fastened high on two walls or standards. Each contestant arranges an apple so that it can be reached by standing on tiptoe. At the signal, each player endeavors to get a bite of his or her apple. But just as one player gets hold of an apple, another player may let go. As a result, the apples are jerked up or down. The first player to get three bites wins. Hands cannot be used.

Variation: **Biting a Doughnut**—The first player to get a bite of a doughnut wins.

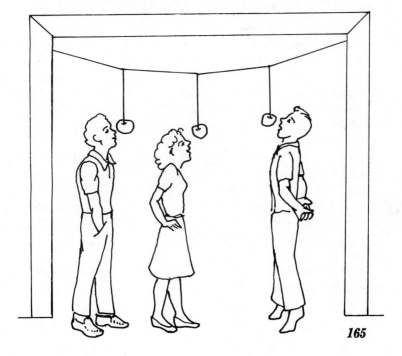

Hog Calling—Divide the group into partners. Each couple is to choose a pair of matching words: red and white, salt and pepper, cat and rat, etc. Blindfold all players and place partners at opposite ends of the room or field. At the signal, players begin calling their code words and try to find their partners.

Human Checkers—A giant checkerboard is marked out on cloth, oilcloth, canvas, paper, floor, or court. The squares should be at least one foot in diameter. Players are the checkers. They stand in proper positions and two captains indicate the moves. When jumps are to be made, players jump leap-frog fashion. The same rules apply as in regular checkers. Kings are indicated by wearing a hat or cap.

Obstacle Race—Two unsuspecting persons are selected as contestants. Obstacles of various sorts—books on end, flower pots, pillows, etc.—are distributed over the course. The contestants practice walking this course, zigzagging in and out among the obstacles across the room. Then they are blindfolded (or two other runners may be chosen) and, one at a time, they walk the course while they are timed. Meanwhile, however, the obstacles have been removed. There will be some fancy stepping, stimulated by words of advice and encouragement from the sidelines.

Feed the Monkeys—Partners are blindfolded. One partner shells and feeds peanuts to the other.

Newspaper Race—Each contestant is furnished with two sheets of newspaper. Each step in the race must be made on a paper. Thus a player puts down a sheet, steps on it, puts down the other sheet, steps on it, reaches back to get the first sheet and move it forward, and so on until the goal line is reached.

Variations: (a) **Brick Race**—Each contestant is provided with two bricks and is required to step on the bricks from starting point to goal line.

(b) **Footstool Race**—Each contestant is given two footstools or boxes.

Bicycle Tire Relay—Form teams of 4. Four tires are placed on the floor for each team. At the signal, the first player picks up a tire, passes it down over the body, steps out of it, passes it to the next player, and reaches for another tire. Two passes the hoop over the body and passes it on, and so it continues, until the last player has passed all four hoops over the body and placed them on the floor.

Variation: The hoops may be sent back to the head of the line in the same fashion.

Matchbox Race—Form teams of 5 to 10 players each. Provide each team with the outer part of a small matchbox. The first player on each team places the matchbox on his or her nose. From this time on, hands must not touch the box except to pick it up if it is dropped. The players pass the box from nose to nose. Sounds silly, doesn't it? It is!

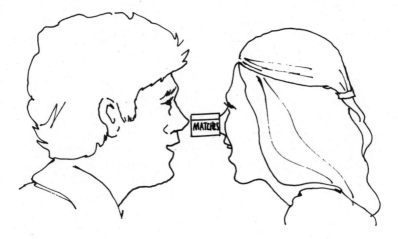

Dizzy Izzy—An umbrella, cane, baseball bat, or broomstick 30″ long will be needed. Contestants hold the stick firmly upright on the floor, both hands on top. Bending over, they rest their heads on their hands and walk around the stick 5 times without lifting it from the floor. Immediately, the players then run to a designated goal—a chair, tree, or post—and back to the starting point. Funny things will happen. Runners should be safeguarded by having human buffers at danger points. Players have been known to butt their heads into hard walls or lose their balance and root up the earth with nose dives.

Variation: **Broom High**—The first person in each line races to a broom, lifts it up and, balancing it, places the end of the handle on the forehead, turns around 10 times, puts the broom down, and attempts to return to the starting line.

Wheelbarrow Race—Form partners. One player grasps the ankles of the other, who walks on his or her hands. In this position they race to a given goal. They reverse positions on the return trip. First pair to return to starting line wins.

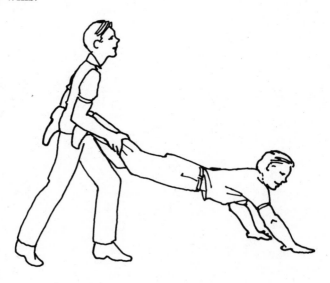

Stilts Race—Players make stilts by nailing a piece of wood to a tall stick. After a little practice, they race on these stilts.

Tin-can Stilts Race—Players make stilts by running wire through same-sized empty cans. They race to a goal on these cans. The chances are that they will not make much speed.

Accuracy Pitch—*Variations:* (a) Players stand or sit several feet away and try to toss playing cards into a container.

(b) Players toss checkers, coins, buttons, or paperclips into a series of glasses 6' to 10' away and arranged in any position desired—triangle, circle, rosebud, square, or row. Numbers on the tumblers may indicate scores. If a player calls a shot and makes good, the points are doubled on that shot; if player fails, 1 point is lost.

(c) **Skee Ball**—Three cans or boxes of various sizes are set inside one another. Players toss checkers, buttons, or beans, trying to hit the center can. Score 10 for the center can, 5 for second can, and 1 for outer can.

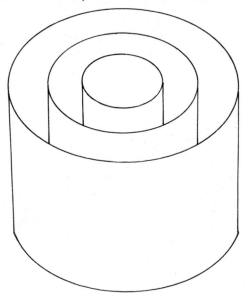

(d) Players bounce a small ball into a bucket or wastebasket.

(e) Players toss beanbags into a bucket or wastebasket weighted down so it will not upset. Two teams of 5 to 10 players each form a circle 15' to 20' in diameter. Each side has different-colored beanbags. At the signal, each player tosses a beanbag. Count is made of the beanbags in the basket.

(f) **Horseshoes**—Form teams of 2 or 4. Players toss washers or silver dollars. Pitching is done as in horseshoes, the winners shooting first each time. Each player pitches two washers. Two holes 3″ in diameter are dug in the ground about 15' to 20' apart. Score as in horseshoes. A washer dropping in the hole, 5 points; washer nearest the hole, one point. Covering an opponent's washer in the hole cancels both.

Cracker Race—Two teams face each other. Each player has 1 cracker. At the signal, the first player on each team eats his or her cracker. As soon as they finish, they whistle. The next players may not begin until then. The first team finished wins.

Discus Throw—Contestants are furnished with paper plates. These are tossed like a discus. Player who tosses a plate the greatest distance wins.

Pushing Peanuts—Contestants push peanuts across the room with toothpicks or pencils.
Variation: Push with the nose. Shorten the distance to a few feet.

Driving the Pig to Market—Contestants push glass pop bottles across the floor with yardsticks.

Potato Relay—Form teams. First player on each team runs across room, picks up a potato in a spoon, carries it back to the starting point, and deposits it in a container. Player One then hands the spoon to player Two, who must get another potato and bring it back. So it goes until all members of the team have run. Team finished first wins.

Variation: Half the members of a team are at one end of a course, half at the other. The first player on each team carries a hot potato in bare hands from the starting point to a teammate at the other end of the course. The teammate races back to the starting point and hands the hot potato to the next player, and so on.

Kangaroo Race—Form partners. Player One goes down on all fours. Player Two wraps the legs about the body of One, puts his or her head between One's legs, and grasps One's ankles. This means that the teammates are facing in opposite directions. In this position they race to the goal line, running the direction the player on all fours is headed.

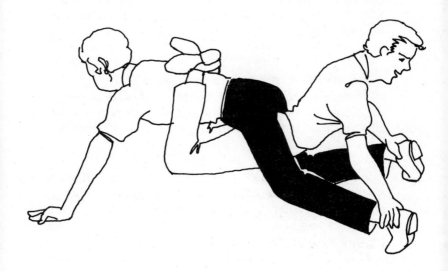

Spider Race—Partners stand back to back and link arms. In this position they race to the goal. Immediately after they cross the goal line they reverse positions and return to the starting line.

Baby Marathon—Each contestant is provided with a baby bottle topped with a brand new nipple, the hole enlarged. Only a litle milk is put in each bottle. Contestants kneel with their hands behind them, while teammates hold their bottles.

Honeymoon Race—Each couple is given a closed suitcase and an umbrella. At a signal, they run arm in arm to the goal, the girl carrying the closed umbrella while the boy carries the suitcase. On arrival at the goal line the suitcase is opened and the wearing apparel in it is donned. It may contain various articles—hats, large pair of boots, raincoat, kimono, bathrobe, baby cap, etc. When the articles have been donned the suitcase is closed, the umbrella is opened, and the couple returns to the starting line. Arriving there, they must take off all the wearing apparel, put it in the suitcase, close it, and close the umbrella.

Marshmallow Race—A marshmallow is tied in the middle of a string 2' long. Each contestant takes one end of the string in the teeth. At the signal, each player starts chewing the string. The first to get to the marshmallow wins.

Marshmallow Feast—A bowl full of marshmallows is placed in the center of the room. Four couples are chosen, one in each corner. On the signal, each girl races to the bowl, picks up 1 marshmallow, races back, places it in her partner's mouth, races back for another marshmallow, and so on. The boy who can eat the most marshmallows or have the most marshmallows stuffed in his mouth in a given period of time wins. One judge is needed for each couple.

Candle Race—Couples are placed so that partners face each other from opposite sides of the room. Each participant has a candle. The boy of each team also has a match. At the signal, the boy lights his candle, crosses the room to his partner, lights her candle, crosses the room to his original position and blows his out. She crosses the room, relights his candle, then returns to her original position. If a candle goes out, it must be relighted at the starting point. Use of hands to shield the flame is not allowed.

Candle Battle—Each person has a lighted candle and a loaded water pistol. Two players face each other, each trying to shoot the other's candle out.

Pie-Eating Contest—Each of 2 to 8 contestants has a large piece of juicy fruit or meringue pie. Holding their hands behind them, contestants eat the pie, not being allowed to push it out of the pie plate. The first contestant to take the empty pie plate in his or her teeth and deliver it thus to the leader wins.

Feather Ball—Choose 2 to 4 contestants, depending on whether the game to be played is singles or doubles. A small fluffy feather is placed on the floor in the middle of a 10′ x 5′ field. Players kneel with their hands behind them. On the signal, each player tries to blow the feather over the opponent's goal line.
Variation: Play on a table, the players being allowed to lean over into the playing field.

Ankle Throw—Players lie face down. Using their feet, they try to throw an object (baseball, knotted rag) over their heads.

Bear Stalking—Two players are blindfolded and one is placed at each end of a long table. At the signal, they begin to move around the table. The Stalker tries to catch the Bear. Both players must stay within touching distance of the table.

Absolute silence on part of audience and stalker is essential.

Modeling—Each guest is given a card or a piece of posterboard and a stick of gum. Players chew the gum and then model some animal, flower, tree, house, or other object on their cards with it. The results may be placed on exhibit.

Human Croquet—Eleven players take the position of the stakes and wickets in croquet. The "wickets" spread their legs. The "stakes" stand upright. Two players contest at a time, starting from the opposite stakes and crawling on all fours. They go under the arches in the same way the croquet ball is played. A contestant has not finished until the entire course is completed.

YOUNG PEOPLE'S FAVORITES

These next few nonsense games would be called ridiculous by some, yet they are games that seem to be enjoyed by youth.

Jello Feed—Form boy-and-girl teams. Each boy lies on his back, covered with a sheet of plastic or cloth to protect his clothes. The girl stands at the head of the boy to get her bearings. Then the girl is blindfolded and given a bowl of Jello and a spoon. Standing above the boy, she is to attempt to drop spoonfuls of Jello into his mouth. The least messy team wins.

Mummy Wrap—A boy and two girls make up each team. The girls are given 2 rolls of toilet tissue. Within a time limit, each team of girls is to creatively wrap its "mummy" in toilet tissue. Judges pick the best-wrapped mummy.

Funnel Drop—Choose warm weather and a good-natured contestant. A boy places a funnel in the front of his pants. Then he attempts to drop a coin placed upon his forehead into the funnel. After two or three tries, while he is placing the coin on his forehead, pour water from a pitcher into the funnel.

Banana Duel—Two contestants are blindfolded and stab each other with bananas.

Shoeless—As guests arrive, have them stand about 10 feet from a box. They are to try to kick their shoes off into the box. If they miss, they must go without shoes during the rest of the party. If one shoe makes it, they wear only one shoe.

Eat a Banana—With one hand behind the back, each contestant must peel and eat a banana.

Shoveling Snow—A large bowl of popcorn is placed in the center of the room, and an empty bowl and a spoon are placed at each team's starting position. The first player on each team is to race from the team's starting position with spoon in hand, get a spoonful of "snow," race back to the team bowl, deposit the snow in the bowl, then hand the spoon to the next player, who does the same. The team with the most popcorn in its bowl after all players have raced, wins.

Stocking Fun—Blindfolded male contestants sit in chairs facing the group. Each is given garden gloves and a pair of pantyhose. At the signal, they attempt to put on the pantyhose. The first to get the pantyhose above his knees wins.

Toothpaste Squeeze—Form several boy-and-girl teams. Each boy lies on his back with a paper cup on his forehead. The girls are blindfolded and each is given a tube of toothpaste. Each girl then stands at the head of her partner and tries to squeeze the toothpaste into the cup.

Twister Tag—Form couples. Partners are to follow the instructions called out by the leader. Examples: Toe to toe, the two try to touch toes; nose to nose, they touch noses. Other commands might include: elbow to elbow; knee to knee; ear to ear; hand to shoulder; etc.

Bag a Girl—As each girl enters the room, a color (red, green, blue, yellow) is placed in the palm of her hand with a felt-tip marker. Each boy is given a sack and assigned two colors. Boys are to try to fill their sacks with the hands of girls who have their colors. Girls are to keep their hands closed.

Chinese Fire Drill—At a signal, everyone is to run out of the building and circle it. The last person back must perform a consequence.

Stairstep Race—The group is divided into 2 equal teams. At a signal, they are to line up by height. First team to do so wins.
Variation: **Birthday Lineup**—Each team is to line up according to birthdays. First team to do so wins.

Scavenger Hunt in Reverse—The group is given various objects that might be collected on a scavenger hunt. The group goes throughout the neighborhood giving away the pieces of junk.

Foot Painting—A silly but fun event. Form several teams. Each team is given a large piece of paper and water paints; each player is given a paint brush. Each team paints a picture, the players holding their brushes with their feet. Team with the best picture wins.

Egg Hike—Several eggs are placed about on the floor, and a trail is laid out through them. As blindfolded contestants begin to walk the trail, peanuts are substituted for the eggs.

Lemon Relay—Players remove their shoes for this event. Each team is to pass a lemon from one end of the line to the other, using only the feet.

Tomato Stuff—An empty catsup bottle and an overripe tomato are given to each blindfolded contestant, who must stuff the tomato into the catsup bottle. The player with the most tomato in the bottom of the bottle wins.

Stuff the Ice Chest—Form boy-and-girl teams, the boys wearing T-shirts. Each boy sits while his partner stuffs the front of his shirt with ice. The team finishing first wins. Teams should have equal amounts of ice.

Toe Wrestling—Choose two contestants. Each removes the shoe and sock from the right foot. They sit facing each other, right legs side by side, and link their big toes together for a version of arm wrestling. The object is to force the opponent's foot over.

Leg Hoist—This event is a challenge for males. Stand facing the wall with the shoulders against the wall. The outside edge of one shoe must also be against the wall. Then try to lift the other leg into the air.

Shaving-cream Hairstyles—Two or more boys sit facing the group. A girl stands behind each boy with a can of shaving cream. She covers her partner's head with the shaving cream and styles a hairdo. The hairdos are judged by audience applause.

Decorate the Christmas Tree—Form boy-and-girl teams, or teams of 2 girls and a boy. The boy is the "tree." His teammate(s) decorate their tree with ornaments, tinsel, etc. (It might be a little dangerous to use lights.)

Bob for Onions—Contestants are blindfolded and each is provided with a tub of water containing one apple and one onion. The contestant bobs for (?).

Feet Autographs—Boys compete to see which can get the most autographs on the bottoms of his feet.

Clean-Shaven Balloon—Each participant is given a large balloon, a container of shaving lather, and an *empty* razor. Blindfold each participant. Player is to blow up the balloon, place lather on it, and then shave it. The player whose balloon is shaved cleanest wins.

Eat a Worm—Not really! Licorice strings are tied together in 6' lengths. Each boy-and-girl team is given a string of licorice. Starting at opposite ends, each eats the licorice until they meet. For variety, have several strings crossing one another like the spokes of a wheel. Partners who break their string are out of the game.

Bull's Nose—Form boy-and-girl teams. Each boy sits in a chair, his clothing covered with plastic to protect it. On his nose is placed a blob of shaving cream. Each girl is equipped with a loaded water pistol. She shoots until time is called. The team with the best-cleaned nose wins.

Milk the Cow—Rubber gloves, with a hole pricked in each finger, are filled with milk and tied on a suspended rod. With buckets between their knees, contestants see who can milk their "cow" fastest.

Knee Waddle—Partners place a small coin between them at knee height (between one player's left knee and the other's right knee), waddle over to an empty gallon milk carton, and attempt to drop the coin into it. If they succeed, they keep the coin.

Thumb Wrestling—Opponents clasp each other's right hands by cupping and grasping the fingers. With thumbs side by side, pointing up, count to three and thumb wrestle. Two out of three pins decides the winner.

Egg Toss—With eggs (fresh or hard-boiled, depending on location), partners line up facing each other, an arm's length apart. One partner is to hand the egg to the other. They both take a step backward. The partner who now has the egg gently tosses it back to the first player. They both take another step backward and toss the egg again. They continue to do this until the egg breaks. The partners whose egg lasts longest wins.

7

FUN WITH MENTAL GAMES

Mental games can be very enjoyable. Much depends upon the attitude of the player, of course. And a good deal depends on the way the games are presented. Here are a few suggestions:

1. The important thing is that everyone has a good time. No one should be encouraged to take the competitive aspect of a contest too seriously.

2. Have all necessary materials ready. If answers are to be written, prepare more than enough copies of the contest and have plenty of pencils available. Other necessary things should be properly numbered or labeled and attractively displayed.

3. One of the best ways to direct a contest is to read the story or question and pause for the players to call the answer. If there are teams, allow one point for the side that calls the correct answer first. Take off a point for an incorrect answer. Team contests give everyone a sense of achievement. A player identifies with the group and finds pleasure in group success, even though that player may not individually answer any of the questions.

4. These games can also take place in the same way as a spelling bee.

5. Always allow enough time for the game to be

completed, since these games tend to be a little slower than others.

One of the fine things about mental games is that they can be enjoyed by one person, or two, by a small group, or a large one.

Many games should be original. Take time to work up your own versions. Use your imagination!

QUIZZES

Nature Quiz—

What tree suggests

> The hand? Palm
> The seaside? Beech
> History? Date
> Neat appearance? Spruce
> A winter coat? Fir
> A valuable oil? Olive
> A well-worn joke? Chestnut
> A good-looking girl? Peach
> The color black? Ebony
> A carpenter's tool? Plane
> Someone in high favor? Poplar
> A parent? Pawpaw
> An inlet of the sea? Bay
> A church official? Elder
> Something kissable? Tulips
> Syrup? Maple
> A dead fire? Ash
> Sadness? Weeping Willow
> A bottle? Cork
> A bouncing ball? Rubber
> Two? Pear
> A kind of grasshopper? Locust

What berry is

> Red when it is green? Blackberry
> Created by Mark Twain? Huckleberry
> On the grass? Dewberry
> Irritating? Raspberry
> A dunce? Gooseberry
> Used for hats? Strawberry
> Respected because of its age? Elderberry
> A beverage? Teaberry
> Melancholy? Blueberry
> A decoration for a great festival? Hollyberry
> The sound of hens? Cackleberry
> A way to cut? Hackberry

What flower suggests

> Four? Ivy (IV)
> A gold digger's quest? Marigold
> A tattered bird? Ragged Robin
> A woman's foot? Lady's Slipper
> A time of day? Four-o'clock
> A good wild beast? Dandelion
> A church official? Elder
> The rising sun? Morning Glory
> An amiable man? Sweet William
> What Pa did when he proposed to Ma? Aster

Identifying Leaves—Pin 10 or more leaves of different trees on paper or cardboard. Number and arrange these on a wall or table. Ask the guests to identify them.

Variation: Instead of the actual leaves, spatter prints may be displayed. Suggestions:

Oak	Walnut
Magnolia	Hickory
Catalpa	Elm

How Many Birds Can You List?—If the crowd is small, each person may make up a list. If it is large, divide into groups. After the lists are completed, the crowd might pool information about the various birds. A bird hike would be a good follow-up. Suggestions: blackbird, bobolink, woodpecker, flicker, thrasher, snipe, chat, catbird, peewee, canary, bluejay, crow, cowbird, starling, wren, brown creeper, eagle, hawk, owl, quail, dove, mockingbird, nighthawk, goatsucker, peacock, grouse, pheasant, killdeer, sandpiper, plover, crane, heron, rail, gull, duck, swan, goose, hummingbird, martin, whippoorwill, purple finch, pelican.

Categories—Each player writes the same name at the top of a sheet of paper, each letter heading a column, thus:

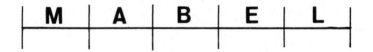

The leader now calls, "Animals," and each player writes the names of animals, each name beginning with the letter heading a particular column. Under the direction of the leader, players begin calling the animals column by column. A player scores one point for each animal listed, plus one point for each player who does not have that particular animal. The leader may call for flowers, vegetables, trees, cities, or any category that suggests itself.

Famous Names—A letter is announced and each player jots down famous people whose names begin with that letter. It is permissible to use first names. Characters in history, fiction, the Bible, prominent people, political figures, statesmen, athletes, movie stars, and the like may be listed. A timekeeper should be appointed and a time limit set. The game may confine its attention to a particular classification, such as athletes, Bible characters, historic names, etc.

Word Snap—From two or more sets of alphabet cards, the leader draws one letter, after calling some category, such as birds, fruits, vegetables, cities, and holds the letter up in plain sight of the group. The first player to respond with an appropriate word receives the card. If no one responds within five seconds the card is put back in the stack. The player holding the most cards at the end of the game wins. The game may be played by sides.

State Capitals—Duplicate outline maps of the United States, including state lines. Each guest writes in the name of each capital. Or call the names of the states and the guests may call the names of the capitals.

Pennsylvania? Harrisburg
North Carolina? Raleigh
Minnesota? St. Paul
Georgia? Atlanta
Kansas? Topeka
North Dakota? Bismark
Oklahoma? Oklahoma City
Mississippi? Jackson
Vermont? Montpelier
Wisconsin? Madison
Oregon? Salem
California? Sacramento
Nevada? Carson City
Missouri? Jefferson City
Maryland? Annapolis

Washington? Olympia
Kentucky? Frankfort
Arkansas? Little Rock
Arizona? Phoenix
Massachusetts? Boston
Montana? Helena
Tennessee? Nashville
Maine? Augusta
Nebraska? Lincoln
New Jersey? Trenton
Rhode Island? Providence
New York? Albany
Indiana? Indianapolis
Louisiana? Baton Rouge
Florida? Tallahassee

West Virginia? Charleston
Illinois? Springfield
Alabama? Montgomery
New Hampshire? Concord
Texas? Austin
New Mexico? Santa Fe
Iowa? Des Moines
Idaho? Boise
Wyoming? Cheyenne
Utah? Salt Lake City

Virginia? Richmond
Connecticut? Hartford
South Carolina? Columbia
Michigan? Lansing
Colorado? Denver
South Dakota? Pierre
Delaware? Dover
Ohio? Columbus
Alaska? Juneau
Hawaii? Honolulu

State Flowers—Name the state flower of these states:

Alabama? Camellia
Alaska? Forget-me-not
Arizona? Saguaro
Arkansas? Apple Blossom
California? California
  Poppy
Colorado? Colorado
  Columbine
Connecticut? Mountain
  Laurel
Delaware? Peach Blossom
District of Columbia?
  American Beauty Rose
Florida? Orange Blossom
Georgia? Cherokee Rose
Hawaii? Red Hibiscus
Idaho? Syringa (Mock
  Orange)
Illinois? Butterfly Violet
Indiana? Peony
Iowa? Wild Prairie Rose
Kansas? Sunflower
Kentucky? Goldenrod

Louisiana? Magnolia
Maine? White Pine Cone
  and Tassel
Maryland? Blackeyed
  Susan
Massachusetts? Trailing
  Arbutus
Michigan? Apple Blossom
Minnesota? Lady's Slipper
Mississippi? Magnolia
Missouri? Hawthorn
Montana? Bitterroot
  Lewisia
Nebraska? Giant
  Goldenrod
Nevada? Big Sagebrush
New Hampshire? Purple
  Lilac
New Jersey? Butterfly
  Violet
New Mexico? Soaptree
  Yucca
New York? Rose

North Carolina?
Flowering Dogwood
North Dakota? Wild
Prairie Rose
Ohio? Scarlet Carnation
Oklahoma? American
Mistletoe
Oregon? Oregon Grape
Pennsylvania? Mountain
Laurel
Rhode Island? Violet
South Carolina? Carolina
Jessamine
South Dakota? American
Pasqueflower

Tennessee? Iris
Texas? Bluebonnet (Texas
Lupine)
Utah? Sego Lily
Vermont? Red Clover
Virginia? Flowering
Dogwood
Washington? Coast
Rhododendron
West Virginia? Rosebay
Rhododendron
Wisconsin? Butterfly
Violet
Wyoming? Indian
Paintbrush

State Nicknames—How many state nicknames do you know? And how did the states get their names?

Nickname	State	Origin of State Name
Cotton State	Alabama	Creek Indian, *place of rest*
Apache State	Arizona	Indian, *place of small springs*
Last Frontier, or Land of the Midnight Sun	Alaska	Aleut, *mainland*
Wonder State	Arkansas	Indian, *downstream people*
Golden State	California	For a fabled island in Spanish romance, or *Caliento forno* (hot furnace)
Centennial State	Colorado	Spanish, *reddish color*. First applied to the river
Nutmeg State	Connecticut	Indian, *Quonoktacut*

Nickname	*State*	*Origin of State Name*
Blue Hen State	Delaware	For Lord de la Warr, first governor of Virginia
Everglade State	Florida	Spanish, *Pascua Florida,* (*flowery feast, for Easter Sunday*)
Cracker or Peach State	Georgia	For King George II of England
The Aloha State, or Paradise of the Pacific	Hawaii	For Polynesian traditional homeland, *Hawaiki*
Gem State	Idaho	Indian, *gem of the mountain*
Sucker State	Illinois	Indian with French ending, *illini, men*
Hoosier State	Indiana	*Land of Indians*
Hawkeye State	Iowa	Indian, *this is the place,* perhaps
Jayhawker, or Sunflower State	Kansas	Indian, *wind people*
Bluegrass State	Kentucky	Indian, *kentake, meadow land*
Pelican State	Louisiana	For Louis XIV of France
Pine Tree State	Maine	Probably for the province in France.
Old Line State	Maryland	For Queen Henrietta Maria of England
Old Bay State	Massachusetts	Indian, originally given to bay, *place of great hills*
Wolverine State	Michigan	Indian, *great lake, great water*
Gopher State	Minnesota	Indian, *clouded water*
Bayou State	Mississippi	Indian, *gathering of all the waters,* or *great river*

Nickname	State	Origin of State Name
Bullion State	Missouri	Indian, *big muddy stream*
Treasure State	Montana	Spanish, *mountain*
Tree-Planter State	Nebraska	Sioux Indian, *shallow water*
Sagebrush, or Silver State	Nevada	Spanish, *snowy*
Granite State	New Hampshire	For county of Hants, or Hampshire, England
Garden State	New Jersey	For Island of Jersey, England
Sunshine State	New Mexico	Indian for a *Mexitl,* an Aztec Indian deity
Empire State	New York	For Duke of York, later James II of England
Old North State, or Tar Heel State	North Carolina	*Land of Charles,* for Charles II of England
Flickertail State	North Dakota	Indian, *allies,* for confederate Sioux tribes
Buckeye State	Ohio	Indian, *beautiful river*
Sooner State	Oklahoma	Choctaw Indian, *red people*
Beaver State	Oregon	For first name of Columbia River, popularized in Bryant's "Thanatopsis"
Keystone State	Pennsylvania	Latin, *Penn's woods,* for William Penn
Little Rhody	Rhode Island	Dutch, *Roode Eylandt, red island*
Palmetto State	South Carolina	See North Carolina
Sunshine State	South Dakota	See North Dakota
Volunteer State	Tennessee	Indian, first applied to river

Nickname	State	Origin of State Name
Lone Star State	Texas	For Texas tribe of Indians
Bee Hive State	Utah	Indian, *Ute, high up*
Green Mountain State	Vermont	French, *green mountain*
Old Dominion	Virginia	For virgin queen, Elizabeth of England
Evergreen State	Washington	For George Washington
Panhandle State	West Virginia	See Virginia
Badger State	Wisconsin	Indian, *wild rushing river,* or *meeting place of the rivers*
Equality State	Wyoming	For Wyoming Valley in Pennsylvania

Identifying Presidents—Cut out, number, and post pictures of the Presidents of the United States. Ask guests to identify them.

Presidential Nicknames—What Presidents answered to the following nicknames? (Add your own to this list.)

Rail splitter of the west? Abraham Lincoln
Hero of New Orleans? Andrew Jackson
Rough and ready? Zachary Taylor
Canal boy? James A. Garfield
Tippecanoe? Wm. H. Harrison
Honest Abe? Lincoln
Rough Rider? Theodore Roosevelt
Father of his country? George Washington
The sage of Monticello? Thomas Jefferson
Old Hickory? Andrew Jackson
Ike? Dwight D. Eisenhower
Tricky Dickie? Richard M. Nixon
Peanut Farmer? James E. Carter

What President—

What President was the first President of the United
States? George Washington

What President had a son who became President? John
Adams

What was the son's name? John Quincy Adams

What President fought in the war of 1812? Andrew
Jackson

What President outlined a foreign policy with South
America? Monroe

What two Presidents died on the same day? Thomas
Jefferson and John Adams

What four Presidents were assassinated? Lincoln,
Garfield, McKinley, and Kennedy

What Presidential candidate was known as the silver-
tongued orator? William Jennings Bryan

What Presidential candidate was noted for his brown
derby? Al Smith

What President said, "I do not choose to run"? Calvin
Coolidge

What President was never elected by the people? Gerald
R. Ford

What President resigned? Richard M. Nixon

What President was a film actor? Ronald Reagan

Quiz Baseball—Here is a game that can be used at a
picnic or party with a small group or a large one. Sides
come to bat as in regular baseball. The umpire, or leader,
shoots a question at the batter. If the answer is correct, the
batter makes a hit and gets on base. Then another batter
comes up. A side completes its inning at bat when it has
missed three questions.

Questions are designated as singles, doubles, triples, or
home runs, according to their difficulty. Extremely easy
questions might be "double-play" balls, in which case, if
there are players on the bases, two are out if the batter

answers incorrectly. The leader should work out the list of questions carefully, evaluating them as singles, doubles, etc., according to the ability of the group. When a question is asked, the value should be announced. A few suggestions are offered here. Others may be gleaned from the other quizzes in this chapter.

1. How long is a fortnight? (Single)
2. What country was first in space? (Double)
3. What is the largest ocean in the world? (Double)
4. Who threw his cloak over a mud puddle for his queen? (Single)
5. Do fish close their eyes when they sleep? Give the reason for your answer. (Single, if only first part is answered correctly; triple, if reason is correct)
6. Who sold his birthright for a mess of pottage? (Single)
7. What animal is king of beasts? (Single; double play if missed)
8. Who wrote a collection of maxims called *Poor Richard's Almanac?* (Double)
9. What colors would you mix to make orange? (Double)
10. How long did Rip Van Winkle sleep? (Double)
11. What was the first permanent English settlement in America? (Double)
12. Who was the father of Pocahontas? (Home run)
13. How many senators are elected from each state? (Single)
14. What Carthaginian general crossed the Alps with his army? (Home run)
15. Who found the "Genesis Rock" on the moon? (Triple)
16. What sea animal has 8 arms or tentacles? (Single)
17. In what athletic game is a puck used? (Single)
18. In what athletic game is a "pigskin" used? (Single; double play if missed)
19. What President grew peanuts?
20. Who said, "Am I my brother's keeper?" (Single)

21. How many letters are there in the English alphabet? (Single)
22. Who looked just like Tweedledum? (Single)
23. What animal in America carries her baby in a pouch, like the kangaroo? (Home run)
24. What year followed 1 B.C.? (Single)
25. Who created the cartoon character Mickey Mouse? (Double)
26. Where is "Music City, U.S.A."? (Single)
27. What animal is called the ship of the desert? (Single)
28. In the Bible, whose wife turned into a pillar of salt? (Single)
29. Does a rabbit run faster uphill, or downhill? Give the reason for your answer. (Single, if the first part is answered; home run, if the reason is given)
30. What is a dogie? (Triple)
31. Where did the Incas live? (Double)
32. Who said, "Give me liberty or give me death"? (Single; double play if missed)
33. How may legs has a spider? (Triple)
34. Which was our 50th state? (Single)
35. Who created Snoopy? (Triple)
36. What is a doe? (Double)
37. People of what profession take the oath of Hippocrates? (Triple)
38. What famous pianist and composer was once Premier of Poland (Single)
39. How do frogs drink? (Double)
40. What mythical giant held the world on his shoulders? (Single)
41. What is the name of the Mohammedan Bible? (Double)
42. Where was the first Olympiad held?
43. Who wrote *Tom Sawyer?* (Single)
44. What famous German composer was deaf during the last years of his life? (Double)
45. In the Bible, who had a coat of many colors? (Single)

46. What is the oldest city in the United States? (Double)
47. Who wrote *Treasure Island?* (Double)
48. What is the largest desert in the world? (Single)
49. What is a bronco? (Double)
50. Do birds have teeth? (Single)

For an ordinary game the umpire would need at least one hundred questions. When a question is missed it is not necessary to continue calling it until it is answered. It might be good technique to save it for use later in the game, coming back to it occasionally until it is answered correctly.

Answers: (1) Two weeks (2) Russia (3) Pacific. It is more than twice as large as the Atlantic (4) Sir Walter Raleigh (5) No. They have no eyelids (6) Esau (7) Lion (8) Benjamin Franklin (9) Red and yellow (10) Twenty years (11) Jamestown, Virginia (12) Powhatan (13) Two (14) Hannibal (15) James Erwin (16) An octopus (17) Ice hockey (18) Football (19) James E. Carter (20) Cain (21) Twenty-six (22) Tweedledee (23) An opossum (24) A.D. (25) Walt Disney (26) Nashville, Tennessee (27) A camel (28) Lot's (29) Uphill, because the front legs are shorter than the hind ones (30) A motherless calf (31) In Peru (32) Patrick Henry (33) Eight (34) Hawaii (35) Charles Shultz (36) A female deer (37) The medical profession (38) Ignace Jan Paderewski (39) Through their skins (40) Atlas (41) The Koran (42) Greece (43) Mark Twain (Samuel L. Clemens) (44) Ludwig van Beethoven (45) Joseph (46) St. Augustine, Florida (47) Robert Louis Stevenson (48) Sahara (49) A half-wild unbroken pony (50) No

Quotations—Quotations are written on cards and read to the group. The first player who names the author is given the card. Or a typed list is given to each guest, and individuals or couples may fill in the proper answers. Bartlett's *Familiar Quotations* is a good source.

Familiar poems and prose may also be used. Keep your quotations fairly within the range of interest and knowledge of your group. They must not be so difficult as to give the group a feeling of futility. As the group grows in knowledge and expertness, the contests may be given wider range. They may center on one type of quotation, such as poetry, history, drama, Bible, or they may be confined to one writer, such as Shakespeare. The guests would then identify the source of the quotation. The quotation might be:

> Yon Cassius has a lean and hungry look;
> He thinks too much: such men are dangerous.

The correct answer would be "Caesar, in *Julius Caesar*."

Variation: Give only part of the quotation and the guests complete it. Suggestions:

"Give me liberty or give me death." —Patrick Henry

"The British are coming!" —Paul Revere

"To be or not to be, that is the question." —Shakespeare

"I only regret that I have but one life to lose for my country." —Nathan Hale

"You can fool some of the people all of the time, and all of the people some of the time, but you can't fool all of the people all of the time." —Abraham Lincoln

"Why don't you speak for yourself, John?" —Priscilla to John Alden

"Here's one small step for a man—one giant leap for mankind." —Neil Armstrong

"Ask not what your country can do for you; ask what you can do for your country." —John F. Kennedy

(Add recent quotes.)

Historical Objects—Duplicate copies of the contest and guests may fill in the correct names. Or call out the symbols and guests may shout the answers either as individuals or as groups. Or display objects or pictures representing them, properly numbered, and guests may move about identifying the objects and making their lists.

What persons or characters are suggested by the following?

> A rainbow? Noah
> A kite? Benjamin Franklin
> A glass slipper? Cinderella
> An apple? William Tell
> A silver lamp? Aladdin
> A slingshot? David
> A coat of many colors? Joseph
> A wolf? Red Riding Hood
> Long hair? Samson
> A hatchet? George Washington
> A footprint? Robinson Crusoe
> A cloak? Sir Walter Raleigh
> A man on the moon? Neil Armstrong
> A burning bush? Moses
> A rail fence? Abraham Lincoln

A College Romance—The italicized words are the names of colleges and universities. Try your luck at making up your own fill-ins. Maybe your answers will be better than ours.

"Man, did you get a load of that *Auburn*-haired girl who passed just now! And did you *Notre Dame* who was with her?"

"Yeah, that's *Agnes Scott* and her sister. She's the *Centre* of attention of the Navy boys at *Annapolis,* a sort of *Columbia* the gem of the ocean," answered George.

"Well," said Jack *Smith,* "She *Knox* me out. You can tell it with *Penn, State* it out loud—she *Drew* me the minute she came into sight. *Georgia* want that girl."

"Oh, really?" mocked George. "But she's good enough for the *Duke* of York."

"Well, I may not have as much money as *Vanderbilt* did, but that doesn't stop me one *Whitman. Erskine* is the skin you love to touch. She looks so good to me in that *Brown* outfit that I'd like to be her *Princeton* night and always. *Manhattan* ought to feel that way, I guess, the first time he sees a girl. But I really would like to have them throw *Rice* at us."

"Wait a minute, man. You can't even af-*Fordham* for breakfast! And anyway, she left her heart way down upon the *Sewanee* River. You can't expect her to be interested in *Tufts* like us."

"Well, I guess I'll go out on the *Pacific* Coast in the *Northwestern* part of the country. Hereafter, I'll lock my heart with a *Yale* lock."

A Hiking Romance—Blank spaces are to be filled in with the names of trees or flowers.

This romance began on a hike one day. It is true that he had met her once before down at the (__1__) where he was a lifeguard, but they did not really get to know each other until the day of the hike. Her name was (__2__) Budd, and his was (__3__) Wood.

She was very (__4__) with all the boys. In fact, (__5__) of them hung around her home. Her (__6__) was afraid she would marry some ne'er-do-well. He wanted her to (__7__) so that she could have all the comforts and luxuries she wanted. She had always said, however, that a girl who married for anything but love was (__8__) crazy.

(__9__) Wood thought she was a (__10__), and he had fallen in love with her at first sight. The hike gave him the opportunity to tell her about it. "(__11__) are a real (__12__) beauty. (__13__) are the (__14__) of my eye." Thereupon he (__15__) to marry him.

She loved him but she pretended to doubt him. "What (__16__) Slipper did I see in your car the other day?" she parried. "Oh, that belonged to my brother, (__17__)

William. It was his wife's," he replied earnestly. "Oh, (__18__) me or I'll have a (__19__). It is near to breaking now. If you only knew how I (__20__) for you."

Just then her little brother Johnny fell down. He did not get up, and he sure did (__21__). She called to him, "(__22__), you're not hurt." "Oh, sis," he yelled back at her, "How can you (__23__) that?"

(__24__) Wood resumed his courting, trying out a little French he had learned at school. *"Mon (__25__), je t'aime."* As that was all the French he could remember, he fell back on perfectly good English. "Let me press your (__26__) to mine." Johnny thought he was a big (__27__), but she thought he was wonderful. "You're a (__28__)," she said as she cuddled in his arms. "We will be married at (__29__) tomorrow."

So (__30__) performed the ceremony, and all their days were blessed with (__31__).

Answers: (1) Beech (2) Rose (3) Red, Cotton, or Dog (4) Poplar (5) Phlox (6) Poppy (7) Marigold (8) Plum (9) Red (10) Peach (11) Yew (12) American (13) Yew (14) Apple (15) Aster (16) Lady's (17) Sweet (18) Rosemary (19) Bleeding Heart (20) Pine (21) Balsam (22) Johnny-jump-up (23) Lilac (24) Red (25) Cherry (*Cherie*) (26) Tulips (27) Prune (28) Daisy (29) Four-o'clock (30) Jack-in-the-pulpit (31) Sweet Peas

Bible Basketball—Mark center circle, foul line, Xs for positions of players, and baskets. Six to twelve players would be the maximum for a fast game, or even fewer, if there are "roving" centers. The referee, who asks the Bible questions, "tosses up" the ball at center. The first center to answer correctly "shoots" the ball by pointing to the forward on his team to receive the next question. The referee then tosses out another question for that forward and that player's guard on the other team. If the forward wins, a goal is scored for 2 points. If the guard wins, the next try goes to the forward that player indicates on his or her own team. If that forward's guard wins this time, the play goes back to center. Anyone who prompts allows the opposing player a "free throw" for a possible correct answer and 1 point. It is important that the referee have a well-prepared list of questions. Much depends on keeping the game moving. To speed up the game a time limit may be used, in which case the ball goes "out of bounds" and back to the centers with a new question.

Bible Quiz—

1. Who caught his hair in an oak tree while fleeing from his father's soldiers?
2. Which of the twelve disciples acted as treasurer?
3. Moses' rod was turned into which of the following: a tree branch, a serpent, a burning bush?
4. On what world famous road did Paul travel on his way to Rome?
5. What was the name of Methusaleh's father?
6. Who is the greatest orator mentioned in the Bible?
7. What boy had a coat of many colors?
8. What was the name of Abraham's wife?
9. What Old Testament character asked permission of his king to go back to Jerusalem to rebuild its walls?
10. Who was the "weeping prophet"?
11. What prophet saw a wheel and is memorialized in a Negro spiritual? What is the spiritual?
12. What Old Testament character put up a great wrestling exhibition?
13. Finish the following question? "Greater love hath no man than ———."
14. What were the names of the three Hebrew boys a Babylonian king threw into the fiery furnace?
15. What was the name of that king?
16. Who was the king of Babylon who had a big feast at

which he saw a hand writing on the wall, the writing being interpreted to him by Daniel?

17. What prophet anointed Saul as king of Israel?
18. What great warrior king played a harp and wrote songs?
19. What famous queen visited Solomon?
20. What wicked queen so frightened Elijah that he fled?
21. What prophet "saw the Lord" in the year King Uzziah died?
22. Fill in the missing word in the following quotation from I Timothy 4:12: "Let no man despise thy youth, but be thou an ——— of the believers in word, in conversation, in charity, in spirit, in faith, in purity."
23. What prophet was swallowed by a whale?
24. One of Job's "comforters" is often referred to as "the smallest man in the Bible." Who was he?
25. What is the name of the woman Samson loved?

Answers: (1) Absalom (2) Judas (3) A serpent (4) The Appian Way (5) Enoch (6) Samson—He brought the house down even though it was filled with his enemies. (7) Joseph (8) Sarah (9) Nehemiah (10) Jeremiah (11) Ezekiel—"Ezekiel Saw de Wheel." (12) Jacob (13) ". . . this, that a man lay down his life for his friend." (14) Shadrach, Meshach, and Abednego (15) Nebuchadnezzar (16) Belshazzar (17) Samuel (18) David (19) The Queen of Sheba (20) Jezebel (21) Isaiah (22) example (23) Jonah (24) Bildad the Shuhite (25) Delilah

Books of the New Testament—Find and circle the books of the New Testament (listed on page 202).
Example: J U D E

```
N  O  J  A  M  I  N  I  B  O  R  F  F  E  J
J  P  S  N  O  I  T  A  L  E  V  E  R  Z  P
W  E  H  T  T  A  M  C  B  P  P  I  G  G  H
N  T  I  T  U  S  C  T  Y  H  K  U  A  A  I
M  E  J  L  M  K  T  S  I  E  S  P  L  V  L
S  R  O  M  A  N  S  L  N  S  H  C  A  S  I
W  O  N  X  R  J  E  I  J  I  T  P  T  N  P
E  X  H  L  K  M  M  H  L  A  E  O  I  A  P
R  U  O  V  O  N  Q  E  U  N  M  R  A  I  I
B  W  J  N  S  H  M  S  K  S  K  E  N  S  A
E  E  P  J  A  M  E  S  E  Z  G  D  S  S  N
H  D  V  W  N (J  U  D  E) J  Z  P  R  O  S
C  O  R  I  N  T  H  I  A  N  S  S  F  L  R
Y  A  Q  T  R  G  Y  H  T  O  M  I  T  O  J
T  H  E  S  S  A  L  O  N  I  A  N  S  C  E
```

Matthew	Colossians
Mark	Thessalonians
Luke	Timothy
John	Titus
Acts	Philemon
Romans	Hebrews
Corinthians	James
Galatians	Peter
Ephesians	Jude
Philippians	Revelation

Find the Name—Unscramble these letters to spell biblical names and places:

1. MEEDUTYONRO _____

2. LOOMONS _____

3. HEEHTBEML _____

4. HEZAHIACR _____

5. SAUHJO _____

6. IREEPSHA _____

7. ROVBSEPR _____

8. TOSSPALE _____

9. LEEAGIL _____

10. NAJONAHT _____

Answers: (1) Deuteronomy (2) Solomon (3) Bethlehem (4) Zechariah (5) Joshua (6) Pharisee (7) Proverbs (8) Apostles (9) Galilee (10) Jonathan

What Doesn't Belong?—Some animals, objects, or items do not belong in these groups. Circle those that do not belong.

1.	COW	CHICKEN	PIG	GUPPY
2.	FROG	FISH	ROOSTER	LILY PAD
3.	SWING	SOFA	TABLE	LAMP
4.	EAGLE	BEAVER	HAWK	RAVEN
5.	BAT	BASE	PUCK	GLOVE

Living Numbers—Two teams of from 10 to 13 players each line up facing each other. Each player is assigned a number from 0 to 9, and, if desired, some extras, such as an additional 1, 7, and 8. The leader calls out questions which can be answered by numbers. The players with the proper numbers rush out in front of their line and arrange themselves in order. Historic dates, arithmetic problems, and other questions that can be answered by numbers are used. If the crowd is large, it may be divided into two groups, each group to sponsor one of the teams. The sponsors may coach, instruct, and encourage their teams. Suggestions:

How many states in the Union? 50
How many men on a football team? 11
How many musical notes in two octaves? 15
How many days in the year? 365
When did Columbus discover America? 1492
When did the Pilgrims land at Plymouth? 1620
When was the Declaration of Independence signed? 1776
How many days in September? 30
How many weeks in a year? 52
How many inches in a yard? 36

Spelling Baseball—The pitcher pitches a word to the batter. If the batter spells it correctly, the batter goes to first base. If not, the batter is out. Base runners advance only when they are forced. When there are 3 outs, the other side comes up to bat. The pitcher may be advised by his teammates about words to pitch. In this game, the pitcher always has a lot of "English" on the ball.

Testing the Five Senses—*Sight:* Place numerous articles on a table: pair of gloves, knife, book, pencil, pen, marble, candle, vase, box, leaf, card case, doll, notebook, small flag, perfume bottle, needle, paper of pins, spool of thread, and other articles. Guests may observe for a moment before the table is removed; or guests may walk past the table and then are ushered into another room; or blindfold guests one at a time or in small groups, then take the blindfolds off so that they may observe the table for 5 seconds. Then each player lists every article remembered. Read the correct list to see who has listed the most articles.

Hearing: Guests listen to musical selections and write down the titles of the compositions.

Smell: Guests are blindfolded and identify certain odors: pine scent, alcohol, ammonia, gasoline, turpentine, camphor, various flavorings, etc.

Touch: Guests are blindfolded and identify certain objects: an egg, a sponge, corn silk, raw spaghetti, soda straw, rice, beans, salt, sugar, flour, sand, etc. Other possibilities are silk, satin, cotton, plastic wrap, woolen cloth, cheesecloth, plastic, vinyl.

Taste: This might be the signal for refreshments. If it is desired to follow the same plan as for the other senses, blindfold guests and let them identify raw onions, carrots, salt, pepper, celery, a cereal, potato chips, crackers, etc.

Observation—From 3 to 5 guests leave the room. The rest of the guests now describe the wearing apparel of those who have left. Many people will not know even the color of any of their clothing.

Variation: Each person writes a description of the clothing of some other person present. The descriptions are taken up, shuffled, and redistributed. Each person reads a description aloud, and the group tries to guess who is being described. The group may also try to guess the writer of each description.

GAMES WITH WORDS

Dictionary—Give each player pencil and paper, and form small groups of not more then 10 players. Each group receives a dictionary. Someone designated to be the leader takes the dictionary, looks up any word, and writes down the definition. The leader then calls out the word and the other players write down a definition. The leader gathers the papers and reads all the definitions, including the one from the dictionary. Then a vote is taken. Players who vote for the correct definition receive five points; for each vote for another definition, one point is awarded to the person who made up that definition.

The dictionary is passed to the player on the leader's right, who proceeds to select a word. This continues until all have had a chance or the game gets tiresome. The person with the most points wins.

Word Building—A word is selected. Each player writes it at the top of a sheet of paper and makes as many words as possible out of the letters in the foundation word, using a letter no more times in any word than it appears in the head word.

The player whose list is longest now reads the words aloud, pausing after each word to note the number of players who do not have that word. Each player who has that word gets one point for each of those who fail to have it. Example:

The basic word is "Caricature." All players have "car,"

so no point is awarded. But 6 players do not have "cure," so each player having that word scores 6 points. Players check the words called that they have on their lists. The next player now reads the words that remain unchecked on his or her list, and so on until all words have been called.

Variation: One player may read all the words beginning with the first letter in the main word, another player all beginning with the second letter, and so on. Players count checked words and total them at the bottom. They also total points made on words some of the other players did not have. They likewise total unchecked words.

Definitions—A small list of words is given out. The players, without conferring, write definitions on slips of paper and turn them in or pass them to the right. The definitions are read aloud. A dictionary is used as authority on correct definitions. This game will sharpen up the thinking of the players and will prove a good vocabulary builder.

I Love My Love—Players sit in a circle. The first player begins, "I love my love with an A because she is affectionate." The next player may say, "I love my love with a B because he is broadminded," or some other descriptive word beginning with the letter B. The third may say, "I love my love with a C because she is carefree." And so it goes. A player who cannot answer appropriately pays a forfeit or drops out. A list of words suggested by the various letters follows:

A—ardent	appreciative	baby-faced
amiable	apt	bashful
affluent	admirable	beaming
amazing	adorable	beguiling
aristocratic	agile	believing
approachable		benevolent
ambitious	B—beautiful	bizarre

big
blond
blind

C—Courteous
careful
cunning
cute

D—dear
darling
dashing
decent

E—energetic
enthusiastic
efficient
earnest

F—fair-minded
famous
fashionable
forceful

G—gorgeous
gigantic
gifted
glamorous

H—happy
harmonious
high-brow
honorable

I—independent
imaginative
indulgent
infallible

J—jaunty
jealous
jolly

jubilant

K—keen
kind
kingly
knowing

L—lovable
level-headed
light-hearted
loquacious

M—manly
musical
masterful
meek

N—natural
normal
novel
neutral

O—obedient
objective
obsessed
original

P—perfect
pleasant
particular
poetic

Q—quaint
qualified
quotable
quarantined

R—radiant
ready
reasonable
responsible

S—sweet

scholarly
saucy
sensible

T—tactful
teachable
thoughtful
thrifty

U—underrated
unanswer-
able
unadorned
understand-
able

V—valorous
valuable
venturesome
veracious

W—witty
wide-awake
warm-
hearted
winsome

X—Xenophonic
Xerxesian
X-rayic
xylophonic

Y—young
yearning
yielding
youthful

Z—zealous
zestful
Zeuslike
zinclike

Variations: (a) Players use the same letter all the way around. If the first player uses the letter A, the others must respond with words beginning with A: ardent, anemic, assiduous.

(b) **The Minister's Cat**—"The minister's cat is an amorous cat," says the first player. "The minister's cat is an artificial cat," says the second player. "The minister's cat is an annoying cat" chimes in the third. And so it goes around the circle, all the players responding with some word beginning with the first letter in the descriptive word called by the first player.

Book Reviews—Each player is furnished with a piece of paper and a pencil. At the top of the paper player One writes the title of a book, real or imaginary. The paper is folded and passed to the right. Player Two writes the name of an author. If the names of some of the people present happen to be used, well and good. Again the paper is folded and passed to the right. Then follow in order: the type of book (fiction, philosophy, poetry, drama, technical); a brief summary of the contents; and then a brief criticism—commending, finding fault, or condemning. No player can see what the other players have written. The criticism should carry the name of some magazine or newspaper. Try this one with a small group.

Variation: With a large crowd, divide into several groups of 10 or more. Each group decides on a title, writes it, folds the paper, and passes it to the next group. Next, each group decides on an author, the members of the group making suggestions. Each of the other items is given attention in the same manner. When finished, each group opens a paper and someone reads the resulting book review to the entire crowd.

Crossword Puzzle—Duplicate these small puzzles and give one to each guest. Or make up one of your own. The player who finishes first wins.

Horizontally and vertically:

1. A web-footed amphibian
2. To wander from place to place
3. Above
4. A microorganism

F	R	O	G
R	O	V	E
O	V	E	R
G	E	R	M

Shouted Proverbs—Divide into groups. Each group selects a proverb. Each person in the group is assigned one word in the proverb. At the signal, all members of one group shout their words simultaneously. The other groups try to guess the proverb. This requires close listening. The groups take turns shouting.

Mixed Proverbs—Place slips of paper with cut-apart proverbs into two containers—one container for the first parts, the other for the last. Each person takes a slip before being seated. Now all of the guests who have the first part of a proverb line up on one side, and all those who have the last part of a proverb line up on the other. Player One on one side reads the first part of a proverb, and player One on the other side reads the last part of another proverb. There will be such combinations as "A rolling stone / is better than none," "A friend in need is / the thief of time."

Variations: (a) Players may march in concentric circles to music, and when the music stops, read their proverb combinations.

(b) Or individuals or groups may work out their own combinations and read them to the crowd.

Improved Proverbs—Suggest that guests improve on proverbs. There are such possibilities as "Never put off until tomorrow what you can get somebody to do for you today"; "Cosmetic fancies alter faces."

Split Proverbs—Part of a proverb is written on one piece of paper and part on another. Guests draw one part and then try to find the missing part. This would make a good mixer to find partners. Thus "A stitch in time" looks diligently for "saves nine." The searchers need not conduct their searches silently.

Acting Out Proverbs—Groups may present proverbs in charade fashion. For instance, a customer goes up to an improvised newsstand and asks for a newspaper. The news dealer answers, "Sorry, but there are no newspapers today." "How come?" asks the customer. "Well, there just ain't any news," responds the dealer. "Fine," says the customer, "I'll take a magazine," and goes off whistling happily. It is easy to guess that this one is "No news is good news."

Contradictory Proverbs—Teams try to think of proverbs that contradict each other. For instance, one side shouts, "Absence makes the heart grow fonder." The other side comes back with "Out of sight, out of mind." Again the first side calls out, "You can't teach an old dog new tricks," and the other side, after a moment, comes back with "You are never too old to learn." "There is honor among thieves" and "Set a thief to catch a thief."

Hidden Words in Proverbs—Players try to discover words in various proverbs. The letters of the words must appear consecutively in the phrase. For instance, in "Handsome is as handsome does," these words appear: hand, and, an, some, so, hands, me, sash, do, and doe.
Variation: The same can be done with nursery rhymes, poems, famous quotations, etc.

Proverb Parodies—Each player writes a parody of a well-known proverb. *Examples:* "Make way for the son to shine. —By a Backfield Star's Mother"; "All that titters (or jitters) should be told. —By Serious"; "A fool and his money make easy pickings. —By a Gold Digger." Perhaps the thinking could be speeded up by providing a list of proverbs containing some of those in the following list.

A Select List of Proverbs and Quotations—

Absence makes the heart grow fonder.
Out of sight, out of mind.
Actions speak louder than words.
Whom the Gods would destroy, they first make mad.
Appearances are deceitful.
Disputing and borrowing cause grief and sorrowing.
April showers bring May flowers.
Birds of a feather flock together.
One rotten apple spoils the whole barrel.
When about to put your words in ink, 'twill do no harm to
    stop and think.
It takes two to make a bargain.
Beauty is only skin deep.
Handsome is as handsome does.
When beauty is at the bar, blind men make the best jury.
Beggars can't be choosers.
Well begun is half done.
The early bird catches the worm.
Blood is thicker than water.
Half a loaf is better than none.
Brevity is the soul of wit.
A new broom sweeps clean.
A penny saved is a penny earned.
Haste makes waste.
After the storm, the calm.
Better to be sure than sorry.
For want of a nail, the shoe was lost; for want of a shoe, the
    horse was lost; for want of a horse, the rider was lost; for
    want of the rider, the message was lost; for want of the
    message, the battle was lost.
When the cat's away, the mice will play.
A whistling girl and a crowing hen always come to some
    bad end.
As the twig is bent, so the tree grows.
Children should be seen, not heard.

Like father, like son.
If an ass goes traveling, he'll not come home a horse.
Spare the rod and spoil the child.
The burnt child fears fire.
Better late than never (but better never late).
Cleanliness is next to godliness.
All that glitters is not gold.
You can't judge a book by its cover.
An ape's an ape, a varlet's a varlet, though they be clad in silk and scarlet.
Clothes make the man.
Never cry over spilt milk.
A guilty conscience needs no accuser.
Consistency, thou art a jewel.
Convince a man against his will, he's of the same opinion still.
Too many cooks spoil the broth.
A watched pot never boils.
None but the brave deserve the fair.
Who the daughter would win, with the mother must begin.
It is too late to lock the stable door after the horse is stolen.
Procrastination is the thief of time.
Make hay while the sun shines.
Paddle your own canoe.
The best physicans are Dr. Diet, Dr. Quiet, and Dr. Merryman.
You can't teach an old dog new tricks.
Barking dogs never bite.
Early to bed and early to rise, makes a man healthy, wealthy, and wise.
One man's meat is another man's poison.
Better an empty purse than an empty head.
It is never too late to learn.
All's well that ends well.
Turn about is fair play.
To err is human; to forgive, divine.

A poor excuse is better than none.

Experience is the best teacher.

We learn to do by doing.

Easy come, easy go.

Familiarity breeds contempt.

He who fights and runs away may live to fight another day.

Wherever there's smoke, there's fire.

Fools' names, like fools' faces, often seen in public places.

Curiosity killed the cat; satisfaction brought it back.

He who would make a fool of himself will find many to help him.

No fool like an old fool.

Every man is the architect of his own fortune.

Fortune sometimes favors those she afterwards destroys.

A friend in need is a friend indeed.

The more haste the less speed.

Marry in haste and repent at leisure.

Two heads are better than one.

Cold hands, warm heart.

The road to hell is paved with good intentions.

Plant the crab tree where you will, it will never bear pippins.

Honesty is the best policy.

While there's life, there's hope.

You can lead a horse to water, but you can't make him drink.

Never ride a free horse to death.

Ignorance is bliss.

You can't have your cake and eat it too.

Rob Peter to pay Paul.

An idle brain is the devil's workshop.

A stitch in time saves nine.

Heaven helps those who help themselves.

A little knowledge is a dangerous thing.

He who laughs last laughs best.

As you make your bed, so must you lie on it.
Love laughs at locksmiths.
'Tis better to have loved and lost than never to have loved
  at all.
Let sleeping dogs lie.
Leave well enough alone.
Misery loves company.
Two things are bad: "too much" and "too little."
A fool and his money are soon parted.
Music hath charms to soothe the savage breast.
Necessity is the mother of invention.
Strike while the iron is hot.
A wise man changes his mind, but a fool? Never.
Every dog has his day.
When love comes in the door, wisdom goes out the window.
All things come to him who waits.
He labors in vain who tries to please everybody.
Possession is nine points of the law.
A bird in the hand is worth two in the bush.
Practice makes perfect.
Practice what you preach.
Self-praise is half slander.
Preachers can talk but never teach, unless they practice
  what they preach.
The proof of the pudding is in the eating.
It takes two to make a quarrel, but only one to start it.
Fools rush in where angels fear to tread.
A good name is sooner lost than won.
Be sure you're right, then go ahead.
When rogues fall out, honest men come into their own.
A rolling stone gathers no moss.
Easier said than done.
A miss is as good as a mile.
Speaking is silver, silence is golden.
Every rose has its thorn.
There is honor among thieves.

Nothing succeeds like success.

Empty wagons make the most noise.

Time and tide wait for no man.

Jack of all trades and master of none.

Though the bird may fly over your head, let it not make its
    nest in your hair.

It's an ill wind that blows nobody good.

The truth will out.

If at first you don't succeed, try, try again.

There's many a slip 'twixt the cup and the lip.

Variety's the very spice of life, that gives it all its flavor.

Virtue is its own reward.

Don't count your chickens before they're hatched.

Nothing ventured, nothing gained.

A word to the wise is sufficient.

Still water runs deep.

Every cloud has a silver lining.

Never put off until tomorrow what you can do today.

If wishes were horses, beggars could ride.

It's the squeaky wheel that gets the oil.

Anagrams—A set of anagram letters may be bought at
most department stores. The game may be played
according to the rules contained in the box.

Variations: (a) **Call it**—Place letters face down on the
table. Each player turns up a letter. The first one to call a
city, river or article (indicated by the leader) beginning
with the letter turned up collects all the letters turned up
by the other players. Thus if the leader calls "Cities," each
player picks up a letter. If a player turns up a C, that player
can shout "Cincinnati," collect a letter from each of the
others, and the game proceeds.

(b) Another way to play the game is to have one player
turn up a letter so all the others can see it. The first player
to call a city, river, or item (as indicated) beginning with

that letter collects the letter. The players take turns turning up letters. Groceries, house furnishings, animals, birds, etc., may be called for by the leader.

(c) **Crossword Anagrams**—Players draw 10 letters each. If the player who has been designated to begin can spell a word with two, three, or four of the 10 letters, he or she places them on the table in order. No player can play more than four letters at one turn. The next player must now build on the letters on the table, crossword fashion. Thus, if the first player spells C-O-A-T, the next player can build on the C, spelling C-R-A-T-E. After several words are down, it is harder, as the players must spell both ways as in crosswords. When a player cannot spell, he or she must discard one face down and draw another. The next player then proceeds to play. The first player to get rid of all of his or her letters scores one point for each letter left in the hands of the other players. The game ends when one player has 21 points.

(d) **Spell It**—The letters are placed face down on the table. Each player draws 4 letters. The first player turns up 4 letters on the table. If the player can spell a word of 3 or more letters, using only one letter from the hand and 2 or more from the board, he or she takes the needed letters. If the player cannot spell, one letter is discarded face up, adding to the other face-up letters on the board. If a player takes all the letters on the board in spelling a word with the one letter from the hand he or she scores a slam. When the players are all out of letters, they proceed to draw four more until all the letters have been drawn. On the last round, if there are not enough letters to go around so that each player will have the same number, the extra letters are placed on the table face up with those already there. Thus if there are 5 players and 18 letters, each player gets 3 letters and 3 are added to the turned-up letters already on the board. The player with the largest number of letters scores 2 points; 1 point is allowed for every slam; 15 points constitutes a game. The player who starts the game continues to lead until all letters have been drawn. Then the next player to the left leads.

Anagrams College—This idea could be used for a progressive party. Five tables are labeled: Literature, Geography, Botany, Zoology, History. Players may play in pairs or as individuals. Players may progress in one of 2 ways: (1) The winning couple moves up; at the head table, the losing couple would go to the last table. (2) All players move to other tables—half at each table move up and half move back; half at the head table would go to the last table and half at the last table would go to the head table.

Players take turns turning up a letter. The player who turns up the letter tries to call a word beginning with that letter. The word must be appropriate to the subject with which the table is labeled. If that player cannot answer immediately, any other player may call a suitable word and pick up the letter. Unclaimed letters lie face up on the table and may be claimed at any time.

After players have made several progressions, they are likely to get their categories mixed. There are no penalties for such mistakes, but of course a player is not allowed to pick up a K for shouting "Kipling" at the zoology table.

Living Alphabet—Two sets of alphabet letters are provided. The letters should be from 3 to 5″ long, on stiff cardboard. Players on each side are given one or more letters, according to the number of people present. Two sides line up facing each other, the players arranged alphabetically according to the letters they hold. There should be a captain for each side. When a word is called, the players who have the letters in that word rush out in front of their line and spell the word by holding the letters up facing their opponents. In the excitement they are likely to assume wrong positions. It is the captain's job to arrange them correctly. The leader decides which side goes first. Where a double letter occurs, the player holding that letter indicates that it is double by waving it pendulum fashion. Where a letter appears in two different places in the word, the player appears in the first position and then in the second.

Variation: Call out questions on history, literature, geography, the Bible, or any other subject, the sides spelling out the answers. Examples:

From what cape do the space flights originate?
  CANAVERAL
Where are movies made? HOLLYWOOD
What was the most famous river in the ancient world?
  NILE
What city was the center of learning in the ancient
  world? ATHENS
London is on what river? THAMES
Who founded the Methodist church? JOHN WESLEY
Where is Pike's Peak? COLORADO
Who wrote *Pilgrim's Progress*? BUNYAN
Who was converted on the Damascus highway? SAUL
Who was spokesman for Moses? AARON
Who succeeded Saul as king of Israel? DAVID
Who was David's very devoted friend? JONATHAN

The leader should be careful in making out the list of words to be spelled to include every letter in the alphabet.

Add-a-Letter—Each player is given a complete alphabet set with some extra vowels so that playing is made easier. Players may play as individuals or as partners. Partners would sit alternately. One player puts down a letter. Suppose the first player has QUERY in mind and puts down a Q. The next player thinks of QUIZ and adds a U. The next player thinks of QUOTA and puts down an O, thinking that his or her partner can finish the word if the next player makes a slip and puts down a T. But the next player is alert, thinks of Quorum, and adds an R. The next player can think of nothing else to add except U, and so the next player plays M and takes up all the letters in the word. Then the next player starts another word, and so it goes. At the end the partners with the largest number of letters win. A player must play in turn and cannot hold out a letter just to prevent an opponent from spelling a word. When a player cannot spell or cannot add a letter to the word being spelled, that player must cast off a letter, face up on the table. The player spelling the last word gets all the letters left on the table.

Spelldown—Players line up in two equal sides. Player One on one side starts a word with one letter. Player One on the opposing side adds a letter, though that player may not have the same word in mind. Player Two on the starting side now adds another letter, but may have still a different word in mind. So the word is tossed back and forth from side to side until some player finishes a word, or until a player challenges the opponent who just added a letter. If a player finishes a word, he or she is out; it does not matter that the player had a longer word in mind. For instance, the first player says F. Player One on the opposing side says I. Player Two on the starting side adds N and is out, for they have spelled FIN. The fact that Two had FINISH in mind doesn't help. A player is given until the leader counts 10 to respond or challenge. In order to keep from finishing a word a player may add any letter, whether he or she has a word in mind or not. If a player fakes through and the next opponent does not challenge, the player is safe as soon as the opponent adds another letter or is counted out. If a player is challenged by the opponent, the player must announce what word he or she is spelling. If it is a good word and all the necessary letters are there as far as the word has gone, the challenger is out. If the player has no legitimate word in mind, the player is out. Proper names do not count. A challenger signifies the intention to challenge simply by announcing, "I challenge you."

Whenever a player drops out, a new word is started by the next player.

Word Calling—Players are seated in a circle. The leader stands in the center, watch in hand, points to a player, and calls a letter. That player must immediately begin calling words beginning with that letter. Proper names are not allowed. The player continues to call words for a period of one minute. A count is kept of the words called. No word may be used twice. At the end of one minute, the leader announces the number of words called, then points to another player and calls another letter. X, Y, and Z are barred. Example: B—bane, ball, ban, bar, bare, bear, etc.

Snip!—The players stand or sit in a circle. One player, It, tosses a knotted handkerchief to another player, calls out some word of 3 letters, and immediately starts counting to 12. The player who receives the handkerchief must respond with 3 words, each beginning with one of the letters in the called word, before the center player can finish the count—"10, 11, 12, snip." For instance, if It calls DIN, the player who receives the handkerchief may shout, DINNER, INDIA, NOW, and get out the last word before It can shout "Snip."

End Pick-ups—In this game a player may spell any word, and the next player must spell a word that begins with the last letter of the word just spelled. Thus, if the first player spelled AND, the next must spell some word beginning with the letter D, such as DENY. The next player must now spell a word beginning with Y, such as YOU. And so on it goes. Words used once may not be used again.

Transitions—By one-letter steps, change a word into its opposite. Only one letter may be changed at a time. Examples: Take "slow" and make it "fast"—slow, slot, blot, boot, boat, coat, cost, cast, fast; "dark" to "dawn"—dark, darn, dawn; "sick" to "well"—sick, silk, sill, sell, well; "rags" to "silk"—rags, rage, sage, sale, male, mile, milk, silk.

Rhyme Guess—Someone in the group begins the game by saying, for example, "I am thinking of a word that rhymes with *play*." The other players begin to guess the word by defining it, rather than by naming it. "Is it a fight?" "No, it is not *fray*." "Is it the opposite of night?" "No, it is not *day*." "Is it a beam of light?" "No, it is not *ray*." "Is it a vehicle?" "Yes, it is *dray*." The person guessing correctly starts a new rhyme guess.

Suggested Thoughts—The leader or someone in the group suggests a word. Someone else calls out another word suggested by the first. The third word must be suggested by the second, and so on. Players may call words in rotation, or as they think of them. In the latter case, the leader will decide which word to use, if several are suggested.

The game could begin, for instance, by the leader calling out "Nashville." Someone else immediately shouts, "Parthenon," and the game is on:

"Nashville, Parthenon, Greece, Turkey, Thanksgiving, football, college, education, teachers, books, libraries, silence, sleep, lying, lawyers, court, marriage, home, Nashville." The point of the game is not to get back to the original word but it can happen.

Variation: In a small crowd, each player may write a list. Then mix them up and pass them out to be read aloud. Let the crowd guess who wrote each one.

Spell Down (Baa-aa-aa)—Players form a circle. One player starts a word by giving the first letter. Player Number Two adds a letter (though Number Two may have a different word in mind). The player who finishes a word must imitate a goat. Players have a right to challenge the player who preceded them if they doubt that that player has any word in mind. If that player did have a legitimate word in mind, the challenging player becomes a goat. If not, the challenged player is the goat. Once players become goats they must "baa-aa-aa" instead of offering a letter each time it is their turn.

Teakettle—"It" is sent out of the room. The other players decide on certain words that sound alike but have different meanings: rain, reign, rein; bare, bear (to carry), bear (an animal); in, inn; pane, pain; sore, soar; fare, fair; dear, deer; so, sow, sew; plane, plain; piece, peace; by, bye, buy.

When It returns, each person in the room is to contribute some sentence containing one or more of the words selected. However, instead of saying the word, they use the word "teakettle" wherever the chosen words appear in the sentence. If the group has decided on "by, bye, and buy":

"Teakettle, the teakettle," someone says, "I went downtown today teakettle myself to teakettle something at the store."

Another player speaks up: "I never go teakettle that I don't think what a good teakettle that car would be. If I had it I would be saying teakettle."

If the player guesses what the word is the person who gave the clue becomes It.

Variation: The guesser is permitted to ask each person one question. The answer must contain the selected word in at least one of its forms, again the word "teakettle" being used to hide it.

Bird, Fish, or Animal—Players sit in a circle. One player stands in the center and, suddenly pointing to some player, shouts, "Bird, fish, or animal!" then calls the name of one of those classes, and immediately begins counting to 10. The player pointed to must name some bird, fish, or animal, according to the class designated by the caller, before the caller can count 10. *Example:* The caller shouts, "Bird, fish, or animal! Bird!" The person pointed to must name some bird before 10 is counted. It is not as easy as it sounds. In the hurry to make the proper answer in the allotted time, a player is likely to get the categories mixed. Repetition of anything previously named is not allowable, and the word "cat" is barred because there are also catbirds and catfish.

Traveler—One player, It, points to another player and announces, for instance, "I am going to Chicago." The player pointed to must call the names of three things before It can count to 10. All three things must begin with the first letter of the announced destination of the traveler. Example: Candy, cigars, and carrots. A player who fails becomes It.

Calling Opposites—The leader calls a word, such as "light," which has an opposite. The first player to call out "dark" scores 1 point.
Variation: This also may be a paper-and-pencil game. Each player is given a list of words and writes their opposites beside them. Suggestions:

tall–short	clear–cloudy	wet–dry
fast–slow	hero–villain	love–hate
strong–weak	loud–quiet	hard–soft
sick–well	happy–sad	bold–shy
fat–thin	hot–cold	sharp–dull

I Pack My Trunk—One player starts the game by saying, "I pack my trunk for China, and I put in Artichokes." The second player then says, "I pack my

trunk for China, and I put in Artichokes and Balsam."
Each player, in turn, repeats all that has gone before and
adds another article. The articles must be in alphabetical
sequence. If an article is left out or is out of sequence, that
player drops out.

Spinning Yarns—Make a ball of short pieces of yarn or
string. The storytellers sit in a circle. One player starts a
story and keeps going, unwinding the ball until he or she
reaches the end of a piece of string. The story should be
entirely original. The ball is passed to the right, and that
player continues the story, finally surrendering the ball to
the player on the right. The story may be a bit disjointed,
and there may be ridiculous sequences, but that will only
add to the fun.

Feather Pass—The leader starts a story and then hands
a feather or ball to some other player. That player must
take up the story and then pass the feather or ball on to
some other player. The storyteller may choose any player
in the group to take up the story. Each storyteller must
complete at least one sentence before handing the feather
to another person, or carry the story on for at least 30
seconds.

A Joke-Telling Festival—As part of a fireside or
campfire program this would make an interesting feature.
Have certain persons primed to start the fun with some
good stories.

A Whopper Festival—Whoppers make an unusual
evening of fun. The stories could be built around such
themes as "Life's Most Embarrassing Moment" or "My
Most Exciting Adventure." For the first half of the

program participants would be confined to the telling of actual experiences. For the last half, let imaginations run in whatever direction they will.

GAMES WITH NUMBERS

Human Calculator—The leader asks a guest to give a number with 5 digits. This number is written on a chalkboard or piece of paper for everyone to see. Then on a separate piece of paper, the leader writes the answer, places that paper in an envelope, and gives it to a guest to keep. The answer is calculated by placing a 2 in front of the given number and subtracting 2 from the last digit. For instance, the number given by the guest is 37,076; the answer, 237,074, is written on the paper. The guest is asked for another five-digit number. The leader then also contributes a number of five digits; but the leader's number and the guest's second number must add up to 99,999. The guest is then asked for a third number, and the leader contributes another number. Again, these two numbers must add up to 99,999. Then all the numbers are added together, and the answer should be 237,074. Example:

Guest's first number	37,076	
Guest's second number	32,309	
Leader's first number	67,690	(These total 99,999)
Guest's third number	12,863	
Leader's second number	87,136	(These total 99,999)
Add all the numbers	237,074	

Now the guest who has the envelope opens it and reads the answer the leader wrote at the beginning of the game.

Birthday Math—Someone in the group is asked to write down the month and day of his or her birth. Example:

Birth month and day	1023	(October 23)
Double that number	2,046	
Add 5	+ 5	
Total	2,051	
Multiply by 50	x 50	
Total	102,550	
Add his or her present age	+ 47	
Total	102,597	
Add days of the year	+ 365	
Total	102,962	
Subtract 615	– 615	
Total	102,347	

The results will show that the person was born in the tenth month, on the twenty-third day, and is 47 years old.

"Buzz" Baseball—Players sit or stand in baseball positions—catcher, pitcher, etc. The distance between bases need be only a few feet. A player from the opposing side comes to the bat. The pitcher calls a number. If, for instance, 3 is called, the team up to bat must "buzz" on 3, multiples of 3, and any number in which 3 appears: The first batter calls "1"; the next calls "2"; the third must say, "Buzz"; then 4, 5, "Buzz." If the batting side gets through without an error, then the fielding side must take up the counting, beginning with the catcher and then going to the pitcher, first baseman, and so forth. If one of the batters makes a mistake, that batter is out and another steps to the plate. If a man on the fielding team fails to "buzz" in the proper place, the batter advances one base for each mistake made. When another batter comes to the plate and the pitcher calls another number, for instance, "2," all the players must "buzz" on 2, any number in which 2 appears, and multiples of 2. If the call goes completely around without any player making a mistake, the batter is out. Three outs and the fielding side comes to the bat.

Players must count rapidly so that the game does not drag. The umpire may allow a batter a base if there is unnecessary delay in the field. On the other hand, the umpire may call the batter out for unnecessary slowness on the part of the team at the bat. It is up to the umpire to keep the game moving rapidly.

4	3	8
9	5	1
2	7	6

The Mystic Fifteen—Each player draws a square which is then divided into nine small squares. Now each player places a number from 1 to 9 in each square. A number can be used only once. The numbers are to be placed so that they total 15 any way they are added—horizontally, vertically, or diagonally. The secret lies in placing 5 at the center and then working the corners with the even numbers, 2, 4, 6, and 8. The player who works it out first wins. Perhaps a hint regarding the placing of the number 5 may be needed.

Picking up Toothpicks—Fifteen toothpicks (matches, checkers, discs, rocks, or other counters) are needed. Players try to make opponents pick up the last toothpick. Players who know the secret can always win. When the secret is common property the game loses its appeal. It is best, therefore, to let players work out the skills of the game for themselves.

Variations: (a) **One Row**—Fifteen toothpicks are placed in one row. Players alternate picking up toothpicks. Not more than three may be picked up at a time. The secret— a player can make certain of winning by always arranging to leave a set-up of five for the opponent's turn. Then, if the opponent draws one, the player draws three. If the opponent draws two, player draws two. This leaves the opponent the last one to draw. Other player must be sure to get six and ten in the draw.

(b) **Three Rows**—Arrange the toothpicks in three rows—seven in one row, five in the next, three in the next. Again a player is trying to make an opponent pick up the last toothpick. This time players may take as many as they desire from any *one* row. For instance, opponent could take up all seven in the top row. That would make it easy, for other player could then take two from the second row, leaving a three-and-three set-up. Now, if opponent takes one from the top three, other player takes one from the bottom three. This leaves a set-up of two and two. If opponent takes one from the top two, other player takes the two left at the bottom, leaving opponent the last one to pick up. The winning combinations, as the game progresses, are 6-4-2, 5-4-1, 3-2-1, 1-1-1; or when only two rows of toothpicks are left, the same number in the two rows.

Stock Exchange—Each player is given a number and a supply of beans. When the "stock exchange" is opened, the players begin shouting their bids for numbers—so many beans for a number. After about 10 or 15 minutes of spirited buying and selling, the "manager" of the stock exchange begins calling numbers in. The "members" of the stock exchange who have those numbers surrender them to the manager. Numbers are called in until there is but one number left. The player holding this number is awarded some prize. Up until the time the prize number is evident, players may continue to buy and sell at their discretion, quieting down long enough to hear the call, which is made at intervals. In the calls suggested here, 59 is the lucky number. Select a number and then work out a system of calls that will leave that number. This can be done by putting the numbers down on paper and checking off the calls. Note how the following calls are worked out:

Turn in:
> 3 and all multiples of 3.
> All numbers containing the digit 1.
> All numbers in which the sum of the digits equals 13.
> All even numbers.
> 5 and all multiples of 5.
> All numbers containing the digit 3.
> All numbers containing the digit 7.
> All numbers containing an even digit.

This leaves 59 as the lucky number that gets the prize. The person having the largest number of beans, evidencing the fact that he or she has been a keen trader, also wins a prize.

If desired the manager may write the calls on a blackboard. Enough time should be allowed between calls for buying and selling. As the numbers on the "market" become fewer, the prices will probably go up.

BIBLIOGRAPHY

Anderson, Doris. *Encyclopedia of Games*. Grand Rapids: Zondervan Publishing House, 1973.

Baumann, Clayton, and Merrill, Dean. *125 Crowd Breakers*. Glendale, Calif.: Regal Books, G/L Publications, 1974.

Burns, Lorell Coffman. *Instant Party Fun*. New York: Association Press, 1967.

Eisenberg, Helen, and Eisenberg, Larry. *Omnibus of Fun*. New York: Association Press, 1956.

Fluegelman, Andrew. *The New Games Book*. Garden City, N.J.: Doubleday & Co., Dolphin Books, 1976.

Fluegelman, Andrew. *More New Games*. Garden City, N.J.: Doubleday & Co., Dolphin Books, 1981.

Harbin, E. O. *Games for Boys and Girls*. New York: Abingdon-Cokesbury Press, 1951.

Rohnke, Karl. *Cowtails and Cobras*. Hamilton, Mass.: Project Adventure, 1977.

Rohrbough, Lynn. *Handy Games*. Delaware, Ohio: Cooperative Recreation Service, 1927.

Sessoms, Bob. *A Guide to Using Sports and Games in the Life of the Church*. Nashville: Convention Press, 1977.

Smith, Frank Hart. *Fellowships: Plenty of Fun for All*. Nashville: Convention Press, 1978.

Smith, Frank Hart. *52 After-Game Fellowships*. Nashville: Convention Press, 1980.

Wackerbarth, Marjorie, and Graham, Lillian S. *Games for All Ages and How to Use Them*. Grand Rapids: Baker Book House, 1973.

Wade, Mildred. *Games for Fun*. Nashville: Broadman Press, 1977.

INDEX